ENEMY ON ISLAND.
ISSUE IN DOUBT.

THE CAPTURE OF WAKE ISLAND

DECEMBER 1941

CECIL COOKE

ENEMY ON ISLAND.
ISSUE IN DOUBT.
THE CAPTURE OF WAKE ISLAND
DECEMBER 1941

BY STAN COHEN

Pictorial Histories Publishing Company
Missoula, Montana

LIBRARY OF CONGRESS
CATALOG CARD NUMBER 83-62543

ISBN 0-933126-39-5

First Printing   November 1983
Second Printing   September 1985
Third Printing   January 1988

PRINTED IN CANADA

Typography by Arrow Graphics, Missoula, Montana

TITLE

Enemy on Island. Issue in Doubt. This message was sent to Adm. Pye at Pearl Harbor by Wake Island's Cmdr. Cunningham at 0500 on Dec. 23, 1941.

FRONT COVER

The cover portrays the Marines of the 1st Defense Battalion with Wake's civilian contractors and the planes of VMF-211. Wake Atoll is in the background. The painting is by James Farmer of Glendora, Calif. Al Anderson and Bob Parker posed for the painting and advised on uniforms and equipment.

BACK COVER

Original color photograph of the flag ceremony on Wake Island, Sept. 7, 1945. Japan's Adm. Sakaibara formally turns over the island to Brig. Gen. L.H.M. Sanderson, USMC, thus ending the Wake Island occupation. Courtesy U.S. Marine Corps Archives.

THE ART OF JOSEPH ASTARITA

The sketches of Joseph Astarita, who was a civilian when captured on Wake, are based on Astarita's experiences as a prisoner of war for 44 months. He sketched the works under the extremely adverse conditions of prison camp.

Astarita worked in hand-numbing winters without heat, in the stench of Chinese summers and in the face of constant hunger. He also had to conceal his sketches from the Japanese, who repeatedly searched the barracks.

Astarita hid the drawings, which were done on any kind of paper he could find, by rolling them up and stuffing them into two empty Red Cross shaving cream tubes. Unwrapped at the bottom, stuffed with the drawings and then resealed, the tubes were as light and soft as the original filled containers.

The tubes survived many shakedowns, and were actually handled by the Japanese, who threw them back into the small bag that held the artist's meager belongings. Hidden in the shaving cream tubes, the sketches traveled from camp to camp as the artist and his fellow prisoners were moved from China to Japan.

Astarita, who now lives in Florida, published 40 of these drawings in the 1947 book, *Sketches of P.O.W. Life.*

PICTORIAL HISTORIES PUBLISHING COMPANY
713 South Third West
Missoula, Montana 59801

Contents

Maps

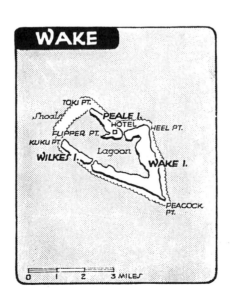

Introduction

The Marines' Hymn, with its memorable opening lines honoring battles in Mexico and Africa, celebrates the history and tradition of the famous American fighting force. To the battles cited in the hymn's opening lines, however, might be added the Marines' gallant defense of Wake Island in December 1941.

Although the fight ended in the defeat and surrender of the island's American garrison, the battle of Wake, starting just hours after the Pearl Harbor attack, represented the first defense of an American possession during World War II. Waged against tremendous odds, the battle always will hold a special place in American military history.

The struggle to hold on to this speck of coral in the Western Pacific came at a time of deep depression for the American people. A good part of the nation's Pacific fleet had recently been destroyed or heavily damaged at Pearl Harbor. The war was only a few days old, but American military installations in China, Guam and the Philippines already had been attacked or captured. The enemy swarmed across much of the Pacific, and it began to appear that the entire West Coast of the United States lay at the mercy of the Japanese aggressors. The heroic defense of Wake did much to bolster the American spirit during this dark December of 1941.

As a strategic American possession, Wake Island for years had been a thorn in the side of the Japanese military. The Japanese believed that once the war began, the atoll had to be taken quickly and decisively.

Japanese military planners assumed the island's small American garrison could be overwhelmed in a matter of hours—at most, in a day or two. Yet it was 16 days after the initial Japanese attack on Wake that the island's 500 Marines, soldiers and sailors and its 1,200 civilian construction workers finally surrendered. Between the first attack on Dec. 8 (Dec. 7, Hawaii time) and the island's fall on Dec. 23, the Americans inflicted heavy losses on the thousands of Japanese attackers.

It was a stunning defense against overwhelming odds, and the battle vividly demonstrated to the Japanese that Americans could—and would—put up a fight.

For the Marines, Wake was a test of fighting spirit; and for the American people, Wake came as a shot in the arm during the depressing aftermath of Pearl Harbor. "Remember Wake" and "Wake Up" were slogans that took a place beside "Remember Pearl Harbor" as inspirations to the American war effort.

While Wake was a battle that inspired Americans everywhere, the island's fall was the beginning of 44 long months of captivity for those who had defended it. With the exception of the Marines captured in Guam and North China and the men taken from the gunboat *USS Wake,* the Wake Islanders endured the longest imprisonment of any Americans captured during World War II. The courage the Wake Islanders showed in the face of the unimaginable hardships of prison camp is a book in itself.

Enemy on Island. Issue in Doubt. is a pictorial record of the battle of Wake, of the years its defenders spent in POW camps, and of the battle's legacy. Many good narratives have been written by participants in the battle and by others, and I have not tried to duplicate those efforts. Rather, my intention is to present the most comprehensive collection of photographs ever assembled on the Wake Island story, with a short narrative to tie the photographs together.

My attempts to gather both American and Japanese photographs taken before, during and after the battle led to archives throughout the United States as well as to private companies and to individuals. The task was complicated by the fact that the photographs were widely scattered and that no photographs, to my knowledge, exist of the battle itself. The maps in this book were reproduced from Heinl's *The Defense of Wake Island,* which contains maps of Wake that are as accurate as any that exist.

I tried to interview as many survivors as possible, but, again, this book tells the story of Wake through photographs and is not intended to be a definitive account of the island's defense. No attempt was made to explore the several controversies that surround the battle—controversies that have not been settled even after 42 years.

Let us hope that American forces need never fight such a battle again. But if they must, let us hope they will show the fighting spirit of the Wake Islanders.

Stan Cohen
August, 1983

Acknowledgments

It is wise for the author of any book on an historical event to obtain the help of those who were there. For this pictorial history, I was fortunate to have the assistance of many individuals who survived the battle of Wake Island and the subsequent years in enemy prison camps.

Several people went well out of their way to help—in particular C.W.O. Charles Holmes, USMC (Ret), of Bonham, Texas, who was gracious enough to entrust me with his personal collection of photographs and who put me in touch with other Marine survivors. On the civilian side, I am particularly indebted to John Rogge and L.S. McCurry, both of Boise, Idaho. They are members of the Survivors of Wake, Guam and Cavite, Inc., and they spent considerable time with me in Boise and at the organization's 1983 national reunion in Helena, Mont.

Other Marines who aided me considerably are Frank Gross, editor of the Marine survivors newsletter, the Wake Island Wig-Wag; Col. Art Poindexter, USMC (Ret), who was head of Devereux's mobile reserve; Carl Stegmaier Jr.; Jack Williamson; Brig. Gen. John F. Kinney, USMC (Ret); Rudy Slezak; Jack Skaggs; Brig. Gen. Walter Bayler, USMC (Ret); and Brig. Gen. James P.S. Devereux, USMC (Ret).

Civilians who were helpful include Joseph Astarita and Jim Allen. Ann Whyte, staff associate for Pan American World Airways, provided most of the prewar Pan Am photos, and Robert Smith and Dan Teters Jr. aided me with the story of the Morrison-Knudsen Construction Co.

Staff members of the Marine Corps Archives at the Washington Navy Yard were very helpful with both photos and written material, as was the staff at the Navy Archives in providing Navy photos. Thanks also go to the U.S. Marine Corps Aviation Museum in Quantico, Va., and the National Air and Space Museum in Washington, D.C., for photos and information on the F4F Wildcat.

I am deeply grateful for the assistance of Gregory J.W. Urwin of Saint Mary of the Plains College, Dodge City, Kan. Professor Urwin loaned me photographs, put me in touch with many of the participants and reviewed my manuscript, offering comments and corrections before it went to press. He is working on his own narrative of the Wake Island story.

Other contributors to the successful completion of this book are my editor, Peter Stark, of Missoula, and Kitty Herrin, also of Missoula, for typesetting and design help. A special thanks goes to James Farmer, of Glendora, Calif., for coming through with another fine piece of cover art work.

Finally, I am indebted to my wife, Anne, and my two sons, John and Andy. They accompanied me on some of my interview trips and they put up with the long hours I spent writing and on the telephone as I prepared this book.

Photo Credits

NA — National Archives
USN — U.S. Navy Archives
USA — U.S. Army
USMC — U.S. Marine Corps Archives
Holmes Collection — C.W.O. Charles Holmes, Bonham, Texas
Stegmaier Collection — Carl Stegmaier Jr., Tallahassee, Fla.
Kinney Collection — Brig. Gen. John F. Kinney, Portola Valley, Calif.
Poindexter Collection — Col. Art Poindexter, Huntington Beach, Calif.
Rogge Collection — John Rogge, Boise, Idaho
Pan Am Collection — Pan American World Airways, New York, N.Y.

Other photographs are acknowledged by contributor.

All maps are from Lt. Col. R.D. Heinl's *The Defense of Wake Island*, 1947.

DEDICATION

This book is dedicated to the Marines, sailors, soldiers and civilians whose defense of Wake Island exemplified the traditional American fighting spirit.

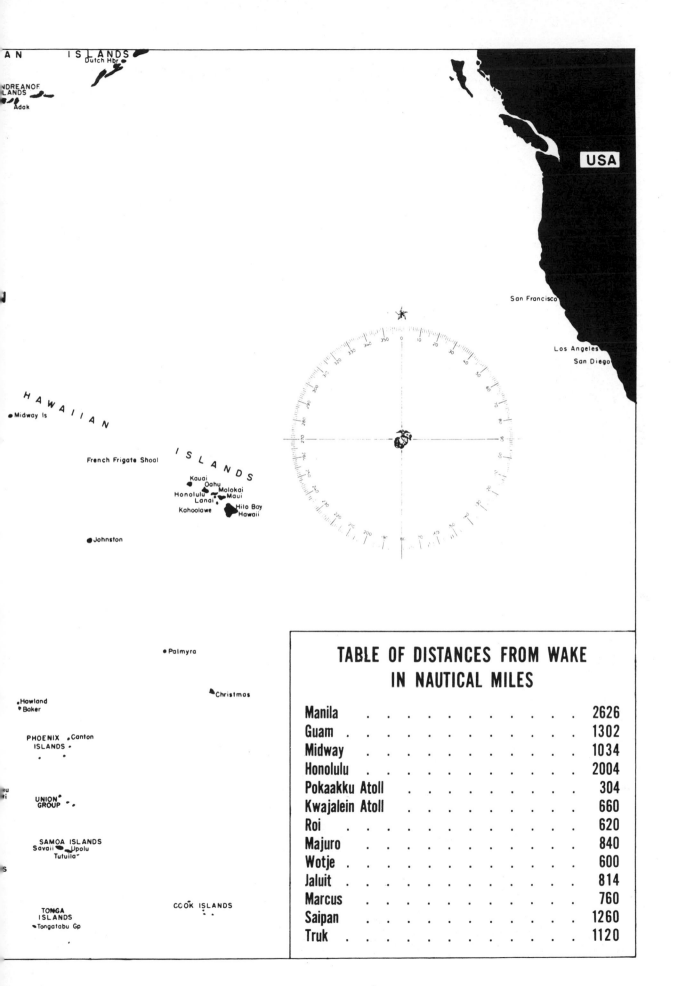

ISLANDS
Dutch Hbr
ANDREANOF
ISLANDS
Adak

USA

San Francisco

Los Angeles
San Diego

HAWAIIAN
Midway Is

French Frigate Shoal

ISLANDS

Kauai
Oahu   Molokai
Honolulu   Maui
Lanai
Kahoolawe   Hilo Bay
Hawaii

Johnston

Palmyra

Christmas

Howland
Baker

PHOENIX   Canton
ISLANDS

UNION
GROUP

SAMOA ISLANDS
Savaii   Upolu
Tutuila

COOK ISLANDS

TONGA
ISLANDS
Tongatabu Gp

TABLE OF DISTANCES FROM WAKE
IN NAUTICAL MILES

Manila	2626
Guam	1302
Midway	1034
Honolulu	2004
Pokaakku Atoll	304
Kwajalein Atoll	660
Roi	620
Majuro	840
Wotje	600
Jaluit	814
Marcus	760
Saipan	1260
Truk	1120

Pre-War History

Pre-War History

For most of its history, Wake Island was just another speck of coral in the vast Pacific Ocean. It was not until 1935, when it became a link in the transoceanic airline route, that Wake Island gained any degree of importance.

Lying at 19° 18'40'' north latitude and 166° 35'20'' east longitude, Wake Island is situated about 2,000 miles west of Hawaii and 1,300 east of Guam. Wake is not far from the former Japanese mandated islands.*

The name Wake Island is something of a misnomer, for Wake is actually made up of three islets: Wake, Wilkes and Peale. Formed of a submerged volcano top shaped like a horseshoe, the atoll has a total land mass of slightly under four square miles and a circumference of about 10 miles. The highest elevation is barely 21 feet above sea level. The atoll is ringed entirely by a very close reef that encloses an inner lagoon, which was too shallow for large ships to enter.

The three islets are separated by Peale and Wilkes channels, two narrow channels that caused considerable problems for inter-islet movement until a causeway was built between Wake and Peale islets. A 50-yard-wide channel was also dredged in the shallow lagoon for use by seaplanes.

Although it is a subtropical atoll, no palm trees grow on Wake. Rather, it is covered by a dense undergrowth of shrubs and small trees, in places almost impenetrably thick. Wake's wildlife is limited to a wide range of birds and a population of large rats, although a great variety of fish feed in the lagoon and along the outer reef.

Wake was discovered in 1586 by Spanish explorer Alvaro de Mondana, who named the island "San Francisco." Yet the atoll was thought to have no commercial use or value and was ignored for hundreds of years.

Its second visitor, the British schooner *Prince William Henry*, arrived in 1796. As was customary for explorers of the day, the schooner's commander, William Wake, gave his name to the island. Nevertheless, the commander did not bother to claim the island in the name of his king and country, explaining that the island "was without either water or vegetation."

The first American visit to the island took place in late 1840, when a flotilla of U.S. warships arrived under the command of Commodore Charles Wilkes, an explorer. Like William Wake, Wilkes disparaged the island's scarcity of fresh water and vegetation.

The Spanish-American War sent a stream of traffic past the island. It was during this time that the island was rediscovered and, on July 4, 1898, claimed as an American possession.

The following year, Cmdr. Edward D. Taussig of the *USS Bennington* spent several days on Wake. As part of an effort to make the American acquisition more permanent, an American flag was nailed to a flagstaff and raised over the atoll. At the foot of the flagstaff a brass sheet, mounted on a board, bore the inscription:

United States of America
William McKinley, President
John D. Long, Secretary of the Navy
Cmdr. Edward D. Taussig. U.S.N.
Commanding the USS Bennington
This 17th day of January, 1899
Took possession of the Atoll known as Wake Island
For the United States of America

*Islands taken over by the Japanese from the Germans after World War I.

Wilkes Island, 1935. NA (#80-G-63263)

A typical scene on Peale Island, May 1935. NA (#80-G-63274)

North side of Peale Island, May 1935. It was found that supplies for the Pan Am station could not be unloaded at this shore. NA (#80-G-63275)

Between Taussig's expedition in 1899 and 1935, when Pan American Airways decided to build a fueling stop on Wake, the island sank back into obscurity.

In the early 1900s, Midway Island was selected as a cable relay station and Wake was considered for a similar installation, but the cable bypassed the atoll.

Despite its obscurity, several ships and expeditions stopped at Wake, including a westbound U.S. Army transport under the command of John J. Pershing, commander of the A.E.F. in World War I. Through the years the island also was visited by Japanese fishing vessels, unaware that by 1940 the island would be considered something of an American encroachment on the "Japanese Sea."

In 1923, the USS Tanager brought to the island a scientific expedition jointly sponsored by Yale University and the Bishop Museum of Honolulu. During their two-week stay, members of the expedition conducted a variety of surveys and formally named one islet for Commodore Wilkes and another for Tilian Peale, the naturalist on the Wilkes expedition.

In the late 1930s, Wake began to get the attention of the military. With the threat of war intensifying in the Pacific, American military planners became increasingly aware of the strategic value of the nation's Pacific outposts, including Wake Island. The planners formulated a series of strategies for countering potential aggressors, each aggressor being designated by a different color. Japan, the obvious adversary in the Pacific, received the code name "orange."

As global conflict erupted in the late 1930s, the American military introduced a new plan for the Pacific. It combined the different color-coded strategies into one plan, titled "Rainbow 5." Essentially, the plan called for the American Pacific Fleet, in the event of war, to steam to the west, capture the Japanese mandated islands and secure supply lines to the Philippines. In addition, a number of small island possessions of the U.S., including Wake, would be considered forward bases and act as a ring to seal off the Hawaiian Islands from attack. Besides Wake, this ring was to include Johnston, Palmyra, Samoa and Midway islands.

The plan was a good one, but the initial preparations for it demanded a great commitment of time, money and determination. To prepare Wake for the plan, the Hepburn Board, a group of naval officers appointed to study naval policies, recommended in 1938 that $7.5 million be allocated to develop the island as an air and submarine base. Yet it would be two years before this recommendation would be implemented, and when war broke out in December 1941, two-thirds of the island's construction had been completed.

In January 1941, a pioneer work party of 80 men unloaded supplies from the USS William Ward Burrows at Wake to start construction on the atoll. Eventually about 1,200 men worked for the prime contractor, Morrison-Knudsen Co., whose operations on the island were headed by Dan Teters. The construction program, intended to last three years, would ready the

USS William Ward Burrows (AP-6), formerly the Santa Rita of the W.R. Grace Co. In January 1941, she transported the first load of construction equipment and construction personnel to Wake.   USN (#NH 83458)

island for its military role with an airport, a seaplane base and, eventually, a submarine base and all support facilities.

As Wake's construction hit a feverish pace, it became apparent to Adm. Husband Kimmel, the commander in chief of the Pacific Fleet, that troops should be stationed at Wake for the island's protection. Kimmel urged Adm. Harold R. Stark, the chief of naval operations, to send troops to Wake, but it was not until August 1941 that a small contingent of the 1st Marine Defense Battalion finally arrived on the island.

In addition, a 58-man naval detachment came to the atoll to ready the seaplane base and an even smaller Army detachment of one officer and five men was stationed on Wake to provide radio communications with B-17s that were flying to the Philippines.

Wake's civilians and Marines were responsible for separate tasks. The civilians worked enthusiastically

building an airfield and roads, dredging a channel in the lagoon, constructing a water system, their own living quarters and other buildings. The Marines' task was to ready the island for defense and to build coastal and anti-aircraft gun positions. But these proved to be very difficult jobs for the Marines, as they were constantly called away from their duties to act as stevedores for supply ships and to refuel B-17 bombers that stopped at Wake on their way west. Not only did the island's defense preparations suffer as a result, but the Marines, who were working seven days a week, 12 to 16 hours a day, had no time for gunnery training.

The civilians helped the Marines occasionally, but the civilians' first priority was to fulfill their construction contracts. Thus, by Dec. 7, 1941, neither the civilian-built nor the military-built installations were ready to meet a surprise Japanese attack.

Wilkes Island in 1935, looking southeast along the lagoon shore toward Wake Island. Capt. Wesley Platt's command post during the Dec. 23, 1941, battle was near here. NA (#80-G-063271)

Aerial view of Wake Island from the northeast, May 25, 1941.   NA (#80-G-451195)

View of Peale Island on May 25, 1941. Navy PBY patrol planes are anchored in the lagoon and a Pan Am "Clipper" is docked at the pier. The Pan Am compound is at the foot of the pier.   NA (#80-G-451194)

Pan American Airways

With the advent of long-range airplane technology in the 1930s, it was only a matter of time before the vast Pacific area would be open to air travel.

In January 1935 the Pacific Division of Pan American Airways was established, and in October of that year the company won the trans-Pacific mail contract.

The first mail flight, using Martin M-130 "China Clipper" airplanes, was inaugurated on Nov. 22, 1935. The route, from San Francisco to Manila, led directly across the central Pacific, with stops at Honolulu, Midway Island, Wake Island and Guam. The trip took six days.

In order to fly this great expanse of ocean, a system of weather forecasting had to be organized, and radio and airport equipment installed in Honolulu and Manila, where airfields already existed.

Although the Martin M-130 had long-range flying capabilities, it could not master the Pacific Ocean without several refueling stops.

The first stop after the Hawaiian Islands was to be Midway Island, 1,100 miles to the west. Next came the island complex of Wake, 1,200 miles farther west (actually east by the international date line) from Midway. Facilities for the new air service had to be established on these islands, but this, as it turned out, was not easy.

In May 1935, the steamer *New Haven* dropped anchor on the ocean side of Wilkes Island, part of the Wake Island complex, after she had been to Midway to drop supplies for the station being built there. In her hold she carried 100 carloads of construction material, sectionalized prefabricated houses, all the appurtenances of a modern hotel, as well as construction equipment. Veteran airport contractor Frank McKenzie was in charge of construction.

Several discouraging discoveries were quickly made, however. Originally the airway station had been planned for the largest of the islands, Wake, but no suitable site could be found there. Peale Island offered the only possible site but the entrance into the lagoon was not deep enough to permit the safe passage of a loaded steamer. No fresh water, food or shelter was available on any of the three islands at Wake.

The absence of a channel into the lagoon meant the building of a freight dock on the ocean side of Wilkes, the building of a short railroad through the wilderness of the island, the lightering of supplies from the steamer to Wilkes, transhipping them on the railroad, unloading them and transhipping them across the lagoon to Peale.

Finding fresh water was equally discouraging. The drilling of wells proved to be futile, and careful storage of rain water turned out to be the only answer to the water problem.

Supplies from the SS North Haven—*and from the barge it tows—are unloaded in 1935 for the initial construction of the Pan Am facility.*

Pan Am Collection

-6-

The unloading dock on Wilkes in 1935, with the North Haven *in the background.*   Pan Am Collection

A small railroad was built across Wilkes Island to transship construction material to the inner lagoon.
Pan Am Collection

With the completion of the seaplane landing at Peale, a regular schedule could be maintained from San Francisco to Hawaii, Midway, Guam, the Philippines and then on to China and back along the same route.

Pan Am also built a first-class hotel at the Wake airplane landing, the Pan American Airways Inn. It became a welcome sight for travelers weary from many hours of flying. The airways facility also had its own radio station, shop buildings and a landing dock for the "Clippers."

But Wake had little to offer passengers other than rest, food and drink. The interested passenger could also walk around the sparsely-vegetated island viewing the birds and rats that proliferated there.

The first passenger flight took off on Oct. 21, 1936, and two flights a week were scheduled thereafter, one going east and one going west. By April 1937 an agreement had been reached with the China National Aviation Corp. for connections from Manila to Hong Kong.

The Boeing 314 flying boat entered service on the Pacific flights in February 1939, and just before the war, Wake was truly an important link in global transportation. At the time of the Pearl Harbor attack there were 70 Pan Am employees on the island.

After the war the airline again opened its station on Wake and continued the service until it was terminated on Dec. 7, 1971, 30 years after the airline last halted its service on the island.

Hauling supplies across Wilkes before the railroad was built.
NA (#80-G-63268)

Aerial view of Camp 2 and the causeway connecting Wake and Peale Islands.
NA (#80-G-411160)

The Pan American Airways hotel and office on Wake Island in 1940.   NA (#80-G-410169)

Interior of the Pan Am hotel dining room.   Pan Am Collection

Pan American Airways compound on Peale Island, photographed on March 5, 1940. The hotel is in the upper left.
NA (#80-G-411112)

Main Street of the Pan Am complex on Peale Island, 1937.   Pan Am Collection

During its first trans-Pacific flight, the "China Clipper" docks at Peale Island.   Pan Am Collection

A "Clipper," docked at the Pan Am base on Peale Island before the war.   Pan Am Collection

Contractors Pacific Naval Air Bases

In 1941, eight construction companies formed a consortium called Contractors Pacific Naval Air Bases (CPNAB).* Its purpose was to contract with the U.S. Navy to build up the defenses of the Pacific islands of Hawaii, the Philippines, Midway, Wake, Guam, Johnston, Samoa and Palmyra.

Each firm had charge of construction on one or more of these islands. Morrison-Knudsen Co. of Boise, Idaho, took charge of the Wake Island construction, dispatching 1,200 employees to the island. Work on all the islands was in full progress at the time of the Pearl Harbor attack.

On Dec. 10, 1941, Guam and its civilians surrendered to enemy forces without a fight. Wake fell on Dec. 23 after a heroic defense and Cavite Naval Base

---

*W.A. Bechtel Co., San Francisco; Byrne Organization, Norfolk, Va.; Hawaiian Dredging Co. Ltd., Honolulu; Morrison-Knudsen Co. Inc., Boise, Idaho; J.H. Pomeroy & Co. Inc., San Francisco; Raymond Concrete Pile Co., New York; Teemer Construction Co., New York; Utah Construction Co., San Francisco.

in the Philippines fell in early 1942.

A long period of uncertainty followed the Japanese attacks: the fate of the civilian construction personnel on the captured islands was unknown. Whether they had been killed or taken prisoner remained unanswered for months.

In the meantime, a voluntary organization called the Pacific Island Workers Association was formed by the families of the employees to learn about the fate of the men. What little information the association was able to gather was passed on to the families.

It was not until late April 1942 that the names of the men in China's Woosung POW camp were received through the International Red Cross. By late 1944, everyone was accounted for except 153 Wake prisoners. It was believed that these men were in Japanese prison camps, although they had not been officially reported.

When word of the first prisoners was received, CPNAB instructed the State Department to authorize the Swiss government to advance each employee the maximum amount of money monthly that the Japanese would permit.

Christmas Dinner
on Wake Island

DECEMBER 25, 1941

RELISHES	Burr Gherkins	Celery en Branche
	Pearl Onions, Vinegarette	
	Queen Olives	Sweet Cucumber Pickles
APPETIZERS	Norwegian Pepper Fish	Chilled Tomato Juice
	Hawaiian Fruit Cup	
SOUP	Cream of Chicken — Queen Margot	
FISH	Grilled Fillet of Sole — Sauce Tartare	
ENTREES	Roast Young Tom Turkey — Old-Fashioned Savory Dressing	
	Spiced Giblet Sauce	
	Baked Virginia Ham — Sauce Demi Glace	
VEGETABLES	Cranberry Sauce	Hot Pickled Peaches
	Southern Yams — Franconia	
	English Garden Peas — au Beurre	
	Whipped Snowflake Potatoes	
SALAD	Iceberg Head Lettuce — Quartered Tomatoes	
DRESSINGS	Wake	Wilkes	Peale
DESSERTS	English Plum Pudding	Fresh Fruit Sherbet
	Brandy Sauce	Wafers
CHEESE	American	Swiss	Brick
	Pimento	Roquefort

. . . . .

Fresh Fruit Basket   Nut and Raisin Cup

Holiday Candies   After-Dinner Mints

Demi-Tasse

The dishes listed on this menu for the Wake Island Christmas dinner, 1941, never made it to the table. Instead, the Wake Islanders were served whatever their Japanese captors wanted to give them.   Rogge Collection

Back in the United States, the dependents and families of the captured civilians were facing their own hardships. They were left without the regular financial support the workers had been sending home from the islands.

The Navy and the federal government came up with several plans to alleviate the problem. In February 1942, the Civilian War Relief Fund was set up, but it lacked adequate funding. The Walsh bill was passed on March 7 to provide funding, but again it proved inadequate. Two other measures, passed on Dec. 2, 1942, and on Dec. 23, 1943, went much further in providing funds for the dependents.

Early in 1942, the CPNAB had realized that the dependents were not adequately cared for and incorporated the Pacific Island Employees Foundation on June 1 under the laws of Idaho.

The foundation was organized strictly as a charitable institution, its sole object to provide assistance to the dependents with donations from the eight companies. Its work was much needed in 1942-43 but slacked off towards the end of the war when the federal government provided better funding. The foundation also acted as a conduit for mail and sporadic information out of the POW camps.

When the civilians on the islands were first captured they hoped they would be treated like other captured civilians, such as embassy personnel, and possibly be eligible for exchange. However, it turned out that they were considered POWs by the Japanese and were housed in several POW camps until the end of the war.

Twenty-six civilians at Wake died during the battle, 98 were executed on the island on Oct. 7, 1943, and 30 died in prison camps during the war.

Dan Teters

Head of the CPNAB on Wake for the Morrison-Knudsen Co., Nathan Dan Teters already was well-known in international construction circles, having worked on projects all over the world. His task on Wake was to carve out an airbase, but time ran out on Teters and his 1,200 employees on Dec. 23, 1941.

Teters was born in 1900 in Ohio and raised in Spokane, Wash. During World War I he enlisted for air service with the Army Signal Corps, but wound up building airfields instead. Thus began his construction career.

After receiving an engineering degree from Washington State College in 1922, Teters spent the next 38 years working on construction projects world-wide for the U.S. Bureau of Reclamation, for his own company and for the Morrison-Knudsen Co.

His career, of course, was interrupted by World War II. After the capture of Wake, Teters and most of his civilian employees were taken to prison camp in China. He escaped once in 1944 with Cmdr. W.S. Cunningham, the overall commander of the Wake Island garrison. On the attempt, Teters and Cunningham made their way through heavy fog and darkness from prison camp to the Yangsi River. Their plan was to secure a sampan and cross the river, where, on the other side, they expected to meet friendly Chinese who would help them back to Allied forces.

The Japanese tracked the two men with dogs,

and on the second day of the escape Teters and Cunningham were recaptured. Tried for escaping, Teters was sentenced to be shot, but was given a second trial and sentenced to 10 years of hard labor. He spent two years at the Ward Road prison in Shanghai, where he lost 50 pounds on a diet of rice, barley, cocoa and an occasional piece of fish or meat.

After his liberation from prison, Teters returned to Morrison-Knudsen and continued his international construction work. For his military exploits on Wake he was awarded the Bronze Star. In 1957, in recognition of his work on airbases in French Morocco, the French government conferred on him the rank of Knight in the National Order of the Legion of Honor.

Teters' second wife, Florence, whom he married in 1935, was the last woman to be evacuated from Wake, on Nov. 1, 1941. His son, Dan Teters Jr., is also a veteran of Morrison-Knudsen, having spent 30 years with the company.

Nathan Dan Teters died on July 25, 1960, at his home in Friday Harbor, Wash.

Dan Teters in 1957 when he received an award from the French government. Dan Teters Jr.

American and Japanese Strategies

In the months before the Pearl Harbor attack, Wake Island figured prominently in the minds of both American and Japanese naval planners. Its strategic importance is very apparent to anyone who examines a map of the Pacific.

Naval planners saw the island as a stepping stone in the vast stretch of ocean between Hawaii, 2,000 miles east of Wake, and the Philippines, about 2,600 miles west of Wake. The planners also were very much aware that Wake was located a scant 600 miles north of the Japanese mandated Marshall Islands.

American naval strategists regarded Wake as a potential base for American patrol planes, a base from which the planes could observe the Japanese islands and the positions of the Imperial Japanese Fleet. For this reason, Wake came under U.S. Navy jurisdiction in 1934.

But Wake's strategic position also could work to the advantage of the Japanese. If occupied by Japanese forces, the island could serve as a stepping stone for operations against the American islands of Midway, Johnston and Hawaii.

Recognizing the strategic importance of the island, the 1938 Hepburn Report recommended a multi-million dollar defense expenditure to provide an advance base on Wake for patrol planes and submarines. According to the report, "The immediate continuous operations of patrol planes from Wake would be vital at the outbreak of war in the Pacific." However, it was several years before Congress appropriated the funds to implement the report's recommendations.

The strategic importance of the island was further underscored by Adm. Husband E. Kimmel, commander in chief of the Pacific Fleet. In early 1941, in the face of markedly increasing Japanese hostilities, Kimmel again raised the question of Wake's defense and fortification.

For their part, the Japanese had organized the 4th Fleet in the Marshall and Caroline islands to seize or neutralize the U.S. island possessions—including Wake—that were located west of Hawaii. Based at Truk and commanded by Vice Adm. S. Inouye, the fleet consisted of a few old cruisers, destroyers, submarines, transports, shore-based aircraft and the Special Naval Landing Force, a force similar to the U.S. Marines. The small size of the fleet was another indication that the Japanese believed that Wake, Guam and possibly Midway could be captured without a great deal of force.*

---

*Guam surrendered on Dec. 10, 1941, with almost no resistance from its small garrison of 153 Marines. Midway remained in American possession throughout the war, and Wake fell on Dec. 23, 1941, after a 16-day seige.

1st Marine Defense Battalion

In 1939, the Marine Corps formed the fighting units known as defense battalions, a new concept in defense strategy. The specific purpose of these battalions was to place a ring of defensive fire around a small atoll or island such as Wake, Johnston, Palmyra, Samoa, Midway and other American possessions in the Pacific and elsewhere.

By 1941, a typical battalion was made up of a coast-defense group (six 5" 51-caliber naval guns on concrete bases), an anti-aircraft group (12 3" guns), a machine gun group (48 .50-caliber machine guns used against aircraft and 48 .30-caliber machine guns for ground defense), a searchlight battery, a battalion headquarters, as well as ground defense. The personnel for a normal battalion consisted of 43 officers and 909 enlisted men. A battalion usually did not include infantry troops.

As of Dec. 7, 1941, the defense battalions of the Fleet Marine Force were deployed as follows: 1st, divided between Palmyra, Johnston, Wake and Pearl

Clarence B. McKinstry in 1938. McKinstry, a Marine Gunner, commanded a 3" anti-aircraft battery during the battle of Wake. Holmes Collection

Harbor; 2nd and 7th, Samoa; 3rd and 4th, Pearl Harbor; 5th, Iceland; and 6th, Midway. The 8th was being put together in San Diego, and the 9th, in cadre stage, at Guantanamo, Cuba.

Wake had received its initial contingent from the 1st Battalion on Aug. 19, 1941. Brought to the atoll by the *USS Regulus*, the force was made up of six officers and 173 enlisted men.

Two months later the *Regulus* brought Maj. James P.S. Devereux, who was to command the Marine Corps detachment at Wake, as well as three gun batteries (each having two 5'' 51-caliber guns taken from old World War I battleships), three anti-aircraft batteries (with four 3'' anti-aircraft guns each), 24 .50-caliber machine guns, also for use against enemy aircraft, and some .30-caliber machine guns for coastal defense.

An additional nine officers and 194 enlisted men came to the island on November 2 aboard the *USS Castor*, bringing the 1st Battalion's total force on Wake to 15 officers and 373 enlisted men. A Navy doctor and one hospital corpsman were also attached to the unit. Devereux had 388 men to man equipment for 952.

The battalion initially was housed in tents at Camp 1, the original civilian contractors' camp on the west side of Wake, and the Marines immediately went to work setting up their defense stations.

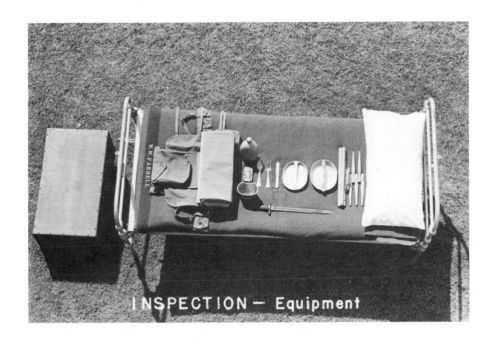

INSPECTION — Equipment

The equipment that the typical Marine of 1941 would have taken to Wake. Called the "782 gear," it was issued to all Marines as field equipment. From left to right on the bunk: outstretched pack with cartridge belt underneath; folded poncho lying on top of folded shelter half (pup tent); first aid packet between a canteen and cup; a knife, fork and spoon and two halves of a mess kit; folded tent pole, rope and tent pegs. Holmes Collection

Battery E, 1st Marine Defense Battalion, leads the Memorial Day parade down Broadway, San Diego, Calif., in 1939. This battery was captured on Wake Island. Holmes Collection

Height (altitude) finder used with the firing data system of 3" anti-aircraft guns. Altitude was transmitted instantly to the firing data computer known as a "Director." The altitude was used to compute the time of flight of the projectile and to determine where the aircraft would be by the time the projectile exploded.

Holmes Collection

A 3" anti-aircraft gun similar to those used on Wake. Wake's gunners could load and fire 20 to 25 rounds per minute per gun. Firing data was transmitted automatically by an electrical data transmission system to a battery's four guns. The anti-aircraft gunners on Wake forced the Japanese bombers to come in at higher altitudes each day, thus reducing the accuracy of the bombers.

Holmes Collection

60-inch searchlight of the 1st Defense Battalion shown in the traveling position.   Holmes Collection

The M4 Director, used to provide continuous firing data to the 3" anti-aircraft guns on the island. Designed and built by Sperry Gyroscope Co., the M4 supplied data to the guns by means of a 21-conductor electrical cable. Targets were tracked by operators who looked through the powerful telescopes (top right and left) and who followed the target by adjusting the handwheels at the bottom right and left. Turning these handwheels gave the instrument azimuth and elevation, while altitude of high-flying aircraft came from the height finder. The instrument could be switched to horizontal range and fire could be brought to bear on land, sea or air targets thus giving the anti-aircraft guns multiple uses.

Sperry Corp., Great Neck, N.Y.

Top: A .50-caliber anti-aircraft machine gun of the type used on Wake Island. The guns were water-cooled.
Holmes Collection

Middle: The USS Castor brought nine Marine officers and 194 additional enlisted men to Wake on Nov. 2, 1941.
Holmes Collection

Bottom: The last pre-war photo from Wake, taken in November 1941, shows Marines and civilians unloading fuel supplies. Col. Devereux is to the left, Maj. Walter Bayler is to the right.
Author's Collection

Brig. Gen.
James P. S. Devereux

The commander of the Wake Detachment, 1st Marine Defense Battalion, Devereux had a varied career both in and out of military service.

Born in Cuba on Feb. 20, 1903, he attended schools in Washington, D.C., Maryland and Switzerland. At age 19 he enlisted in the Marine Corps and two years later, in 1925, was commissioned a second lieutenant.

His early career took him to duty stations at Norfolk, Philadelphia, Washington, D.C., Quantico, New York, Cuba and Nicaragua. In 1927 he was promoted to first lieutenant and sent to China, where his duties included the command of the Mounted Detachment of the Legation Guard at Peking.

An expert horseman, Devereux was associated with mounted activities at many of his duty stations.

During the 1930s, he was promoted to captain and stationed at Quantico, Fort Monroe and San Diego, as well as on board the *U.S.S. Utah*.

With war looming in the Pacific, Devereux was sent to Pearl Harbor in January 1941. Shortly thereafter, Devereux and the 388 men he commanded in the 1st Marine Defense Battalion were sent to Wake Island.

After the surrender of Wake on Dec. 23, 1941, Devereux spent three and one-half years in enemy prisons, and was released from captivity on Japan's Hokkaido Island in September 1945. While a prisoner of war he was promoted to lieutenant colonel but the promotion did not take effect until his release. He assumed the rank of colonel in January 1946.

He was granted a well-deserved rehabilitation leave upon his release and then reported to Quantico as a student in the senior course of the Marines' Amphibious Warfare School. Completing his studies in 1947, he was detailed to the 1st Marine Division at Camp Pendleton, where he retired from active duty on Aug. 1, 1948.

Devereux advanced to his present rank of brigadier general upon his retirement. He holds the Navy Cross; Presidential Unit Citation with one star, Wake Island, 1941; Second Nicara-
guan Campaign Medal, Nicaragua, 1927-29; Yangtze Service Medal, China, 1930; Wake Island Clasp and Silver "W"; American Defense Service Medal with Base Clasp and one Bronze Star; Asiatic-Pacific Campaign Medal with one Bronze Star; and the World War II Victory Medal.

Devereux's retirement did not last long. He was elected by Maryland voters to the U.S. House of Representatives, and served four terms. On a congressional trip around the world he returned to the scene of battle on Wake and to Japan. After retiring from Congress he served as the director of public safety for the state of Maryland.

The general's first wife, Mary, died while he was a prisoner and his second wife, Rachel Cooke, died in 1977. He has three sons, Patrick, John Pierre and Francis Irving Cooke. In 1978 he married Edna Burnside Howard and they reside in Ruxtan, Md.

Floats support a pipeline carrying gasoline to tanks ashore Wake Island, November 1941.   Author's Collection

VMF-211 and VMA-211

The VMF-211, the Marine attack squadron that provided the air defense of Wake, has a long history that ranges from biplane flights over California to jet fighters over Vietnam.

Originally named VF Squadron 4M, the squadron was created in June 1937 and was first based at NAS San Diego, where it used the Grumman F-3F biplane fighter. In 1941, after moving to Ewa MCAS in Hawaii, the squadron was redesignated VMF-211 and switched from biplanes to the Grumman F4F-3 Wildcat. It was attached to Marine Aircraft Group 2, 2nd Marine Aircraft Wing.

Late in 1941 VMF-211 headed for Wake. On November 28, 12 F4F-3s were flown aboard the *USS Enterprise* at Pearl Harbor and transported to the island. Under the command of Maj. Paul A. Putnam, the planes flew off the *Enterprise* on December 4 and were escorted to the base on Wake by a Navy PBY. The pilots were welcomed to the island's new airfield by a committee of Marines and civilian construction workers.

The pilots were:

Maj. Paul A. Putnam	Commanding
*Capt. Henry T. Elrod	Executive
Capt. Herbert C. Freuler	Gunnery/Ordnance
Capt. Frank C. Tharin	Flight
*1st Lt. George Graves	Engineering
*2nd Lt. Carl R. Davidson	Asst. Gunnery
*2nd Lt. Frank J. Holden	Asst. Material
2nd Lt. John F. Kinney	Material/Asst. Engineering
2nd Lt. David D. Kliewer	Communications
2nd Lt. Henry G. Webb	Asst. Flight
*2nd Lt. Robert J. Conderman	Ground Maintenance
T/Sgt. William J. Hamilton	Asst. Communications
S/Sgt. Robert O. Arthur	Asst. Communications

*Killed during the battle.

In addition to the 10 commissioned and two enlisted pilots, Putnam had under his command a ground crew of 49 men.

After the squadron lost all 12 fighters in the defense of Wake and after the island surrendered on December 23, the squadron's rear echelon in Hawaii was transferred to Palmyra Island, where it adopted the name "Wake Island Avengers" in memory of its dead and captured members. Flying the F-4U Corsair for the duration of the war, the squadron participated in the campaigns at Treasury-Bougainville, the Bismarcks, the Northern Solomons, Leyte, Luzon and in the southern Philippines.

After the war, VMF-211 took part in the occupation of China, returning in 1949 to the U.S., where it was based in North Carolina. In July 1952, while operating from the *USS Coral Sea*, the squadron was redesignated VMA-211. It received its first A-4 Skyhawk in 1957 and the following year moved to El Toro MCAS, Calif.

The squadron moved to Japan in October 1965 and later that year began the first of four deployments to Vietnam. Returning to El Toro in 1976, the squadron replaced its old A-4Es with new A-4Ms. It was sent back to MCAS Iwakuni, Japan, for one year, returning in 1980 to El Toro, where it was stationed as of 1983.

According to some reports, the pilots of VMF-211 on Wake may have exacted some retribution from the Japanese for the bombing of Pearl Harbor.

On Dec. 22, 1941, Wake's last two serviceable Wildcats engaged planes from the *Soryu* and *Hiryu*, the two Japanese carriers that stopped in the vicinity of Wake on their return from the Pearl Harbor attack. VMF-211's Capt. Herbert C. Freuler shot down two of the enemy aircraft, which at the time were thought to be Zero fighters.

But reports later obtained from the Japanese showed the plane to be a torpedo-bomber. The crew of this Japanese plane had been credited with sinking the battleship *Arizona* at Pearl Harbor.

Emblem of VMA-211, the "Wake Island Avengers," currently stationed at El Toro MCAS. The emblem's background is yellow, while the outline of Wake and the lion are a bright red. The lettering is black.

USS Enterprise *(CV-6), the carrier that delivered 12 F4F Wildcats to Wake Island four days before the Pearl Harbor attack. This action probably saved the* Enterprise *from being sunk at Pearl Harbor.*　　USN (#N-200)

Maj. Paul Putnam in 1939. Putnam commanded VMF-211 on Wake. USMC (SN-1165)

Maj. Gen. Frank Tharin in 1962. One of the senior pilots of VMF-211, he served in many Marine Corps stations after the war, achieving the rank of lieutenant general. USMC

Col. Paul Putnam. He won his wings in 1939, after he had been stationed in Nicaragua in the 1930s. After the war, Putnam served at various Marine Corps stations and the Pentagon, retiring in 1956 as a brigadier general. He died in 1982. USMC

Lt. John F. Kinney of VMF-211 poses at Ewa MCAS, Hawaii, in November 1941. Within a month he would be taking part in the desperate battle for Wake. Kinney Collection

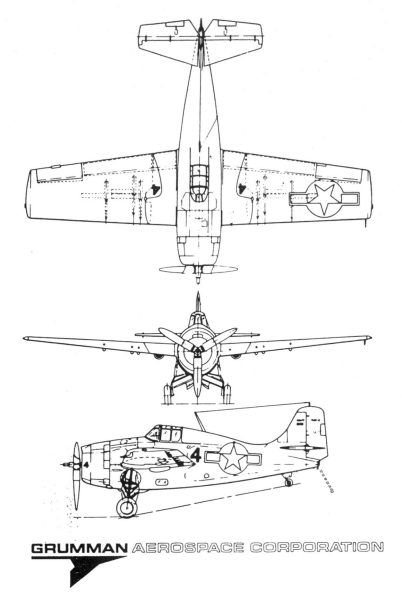

GRUMMAN AEROSPACE CORPORATION

A Grumman F4F-3 Wildcat, the type of plane used in the defense of the island.   San Diego Air and Space Museum

The Grumman F4F Wildcat

With its fine performance during Wake's defense, the F4F claimed a prominent place in aviation history. It went on to chalk up an impressive win-loss record against Japanese aircraft.

Introduced in 1936 in the form of the XF4F-2, the F4F was the first monoplane design of the Grumman Aircraft Co., which for many years had built the F3F biplane, formerly one of the Navy's main carrier-based fighters.

The first prototype of the XF4F-2 took to the air in September 1937 and in February 1939 an improved model, the XF4F-3, was unveiled and ordered into production. The British Royal Navy put the F4F into service before the U.S. Navy; it was not until 1941 that the U.S. Navy and Marine Corps used the new plane. The British called the plane Martlet 1, and, flown by Royal Navy pilots, it was the first plane of American design to enter combat against the Germans.

By the time of the Pearl Harbor attack, five Marine squadrons had been equipped with the F4F-3. Only four days before the attack, Marine Fighter Squadron VMF-211 and its F4Fs had been brought to Wake by the aircraft carrier *Enterprise*.

Throughout the early Pacific Theater campaigns, the F4F-3 and the F4F-4 (which had heavier armament and fold-back wings) were the main carrier-based fighter aircraft of both the U.S. Navy and Marines. With a design that was contemporary with that of the famed Japanese Zero-Sen, the F4F was inferior to the Zero in several respects, but was able to hold its own due to its superior armament, rugged construction and a superb engine.

Yet the plane carried neither armor nor radio homing devices, and its gas tanks were not self-sealing. Although the VMF-211 pilots were well-trained, none of them had more than 30 hours flying time in the Wildcat and they had not practiced dropping bombs from the plane or firing its guns. Despite these problems, the F4F's ratio of victories to losses in air combat against the Japanese was almost seven to one.

In all, about 8,000 F4Fs were built for service with United States and British forces.

F4F-3 Specifications

Crew: 1
Powerplant: 1,200-horsepower Pratt and Whitney R-1830-76 Twin Wasp, 14-cylinder radial, air-cooled
Wingspan: 38'
Length: 28' 9"
Height: 11' 10"
Weight: 7,000 pounds
Maximum speed: 331 mph at 21,300 feet
Ceiling: 37,500 feet
Range: 845 miles
Armament: four machine guns, 200 pounds of bombs

Capt. Henry T. Elrod

The first Medal of Honor given to a Marine airman during World War II went to Capt. Henry T. Elrod for his actions in defense of Wake Island. Elrod died in the battle, and the medal was given posthumously.

Born in Georgia in 1905, Elrod enlisted in the Marine Corps in 1927 and was appointed a second lieutenant in 1931. He spent about a year at the Marine Corps Basic School in Philadelphia and as a student aviator at the Marine Barracks there. He was then ordered to the Naval Station at Pensacola, where he won his wings in 1935.

In July 1938, Elrod was transferred to the Naval Air Station at San Diego, where he served as a squadron material, parachute and personnel officer. In January 1941 he was transferred to Hawaii and VMF-211.

During the defense of Wake, Elrod's gallantry took him far beyond the call of duty. On Dec. 10, he single-handedly attacked a flight of 22 enemy planes, shooting down two. He bombed and strafed enemy ships from a low altitude, becoming the first man to sink a major warship with small-caliber bombs delivered from a fighter-type aircraft.

When his plane was destroyed by enemy fire, Elrod organized a unit of ground troops into a beach defense. The unit repulsed repeated Japanese attacks, but Elrod fell—mortally wounded.

The Medal of Honor, presented to Elrod's widow on Nov. 8, 1946, was a fitting tribute to Elrod's performance during the last days of the defense of Wake Island.

The citation for Elrod's Medal of Honor reads as follows:

For conspicuous gallantry and intrepidity at the risk of his life above and beyond the call of duty while attached to Marine Fighting Squadron TWO HUNDRED ELEVEN, during action against enemy Japanese land, surface and aerial units at Wake Island, from 8 to 23 December 1941. Engaging vastly superior forces of enemy bombers and warships on 9 and 12 December, Captain Elrod shot down two of a flight of twenty-two hostile planes and, executing repeated bombing and strafing runs at extremely low altitude and close range, succeeded in inflicting deadly damage upon a large Japanese vessel, thereby sinking the first major warship to be destroyed by small caliber bombs delivered from a fighter-type aircraft. When his plane was disabled by hostile fire and no other ships were operative, Captain Elrod assumed command of one flank of the line set up in defiance of the enemy landing and, conducting a brilliant defense, enabled his men to hold their positions and repulse determined Japanese attacks, repeatedly proceeding through intense hostile fusillades to provide covering fire for unarmed ammunition carriers. Capturing an automatic weapon during one enemy rush in force, he gave his own firearm to one of his men and fought on vigorously against the Japanese. Responsible in a large measure for the strength of his sector's gallant resistance, on 23 December, Captain Elrod led his men with bold aggressiveness until he fell mortally wounded. His superb skill as a pilot, daring leadership and unswerving devotion to duty distinguished him among the defenders of Wake Island, and his valiant conduct reflects the highest credit upon himself and the United States Naval Service. He gallantly gave his life for his country. *

---

*This citation has the dates of his action wrong.

The Battle
First Phase: Dec. 8-11, 1941

The war came to Wake as quickly and surprisingly as it had come to Pearl Harbor. Like the Pearl Harbor residents, the Wake Islanders didn't know they were about to be attacked until they saw enemy planes flying over the atoll.

Back in November, as the political situation in the Pacific grew more tense by the day, the Wake Island garrison had received a warning: "International situation dictates you should be on the alert." But defense preparations on Wake were still far from complete by the time of the attack.

The civilian contractors were still working on the airfield, dredging the lagoon and building other facilities. Devereux's command had set up coastal defenses at most of the major points of land on the three islets, but Devereux did not have personnel or fire control equipment for all the guns. His meager forces simply had too much area to cover.

There were also problems with Wake's air cover. On Dec. 2, a group of 12 PBYs had flown to Wake to cover the arrival of VMF-211, but the PBYs stayed only a few days and left before Dec. 7. VMF-211 was patrolling the island from the air with its 12 F4F Wildcats. All these planes were in working order, but the island had no revetments in which to protect the planes while they were on the ground, and airfield and parking ramps for the Wildcats had not been completed. Furthermore, when the planes arrived on the island, their bomb racks were not releasing bombs properly. Some jury-rigging solved this, and the planes would prove their worth on Dec. 11.

Another problem was the communications system and the lack of radar that could warn of approaching planes or ships. The island's early warning system consisted of a visual observation point atop the 50-foot watertank at Camp 1. Communications be-

tween the batteries and Wake's headquarters were mostly by above-ground telephone wires, a situation that would be troublesome during the course of battle.

For the most part, supplies on the island were adequate, although ammunition and aviation ordnance was limited and about 20 percent of the island's military personnel were without arms. But the island's supplies included over one million gallons of water and plenty of food for both civilians and military personnel.

As of Dec. 7, personnel on the island were as follows: 1st Marine Defense Battalion, 15 officers and 373 enlisted men; VMF-211, 12 officers and 49 enlisted men; U.S. Naval Air Station, 10 officers and 58 enlisted men; U.S. Army Air Corps, one officer and five enlisted men. In addition, two American submarines, the *Triton* and the *Tambor*, were patrolling in the vicinity of Wake, and civilian contractors on the island numbered approximately 1,200. Pan Am employees, including 70 Chamorros (residents of Guam), also were stationed on the island.

As the senior naval officer on Wake, Cmdr. W.S. Cunningham was the over-all commander of the island's military garrison, Maj. James P.S. Devereux commanded the island's detachment of the 1st Marine Defense Battalion, the main military force on Wake, and Maj. Paul Putnam was in charge of VMF-211, which was basically an independent command.

On Sunday, Dec. 7, 1941,* the Marines took a well-deserved day off, and Monday, Dec. 8, was to be another busy work day. At 0650 Monday, however, Wake received a message stating that the Japanese were attacking Pearl Harbor. The war, which every-

---

*Wake is west of the international date line. When it was Sunday, Dec. 7 on Wake the Pearl Harbor attack was still a day away.

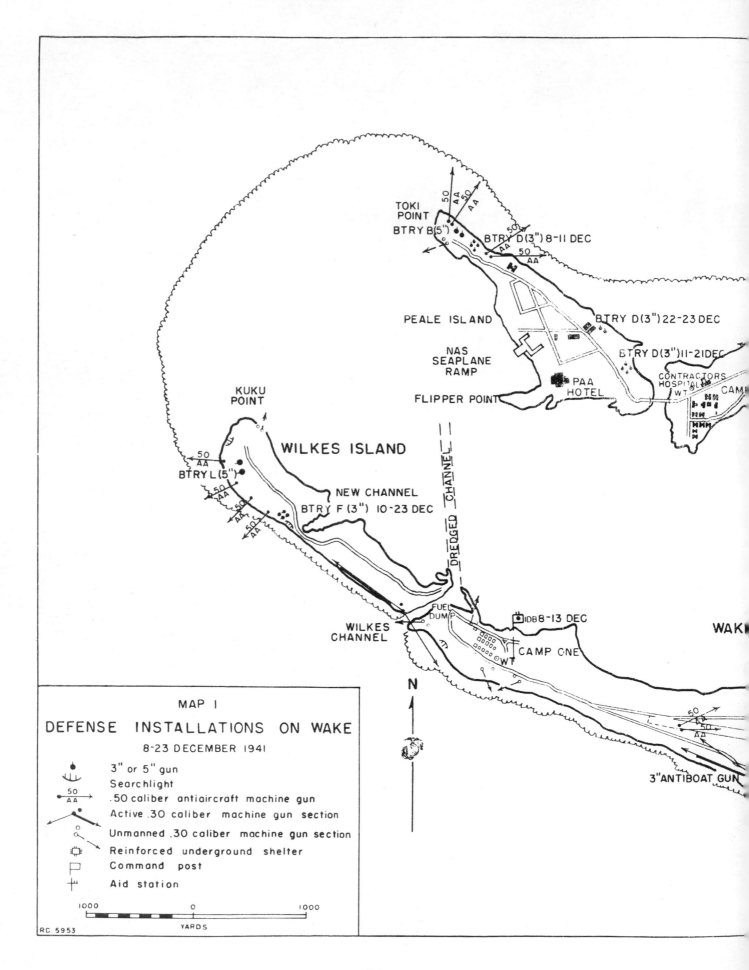

TOKI
POINT
BTRY B(5")
BTRY D(3") 8-11 DEC
50
AA

PEALE ISLAND

BTRY D(3") 22-23 DEC

NAS
SEAPLANE
RAMP

BTRY D(3") 11-21 DEC

CONTRACTORS
HOSPITAL
WT

PAA
HOTEL

FLIPPER POINT

KUKU
POINT

WILKES ISLAND

50
AA

BTRY L(5")

50
AA

50
AA

NEW CHANNEL
BTRY F (3") 10-23 DEC

DREDGED CHANNEL

FUEL
DUMP

IDB 8-13 DEC

CAMP ONE
WT

WILKES
CHANNEL

WAK

N

MAP I

DEFENSE INSTALLATIONS ON WAKE

8-23 DECEMBER 1941

- 3" or 5" gun
- Searchlight
- .50 caliber antiaircraft machine gun
- Active .30 caliber machine gun section
- Unmanned .30 caliber machine gun section
- Reinforced underground shelter
- Command post
- Aid station

50
AA

3"ANTIBOAT GUN

1000   0   1000
YARDS

RC 5953

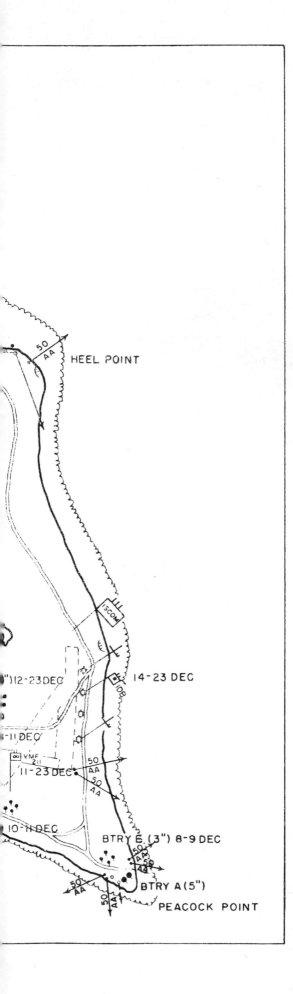

one knew was coming, had finally arrived.

A Pan Am "Clipper" that had left the island earlier in the morning was recalled. At first it was suggested that the plane be used to patrol the island, but this never was carried out. All military personnel were put on alert and issued the arms that were available. To the degree possible, the garrison manned the island's coastal and anti-aircraft guns, and command posts were set up in the bush for Devereux and Cunningham.

VMF-211 sent four Wildcats up to 12,000 feet to patrol for enemy aircraft. But, unbeknownst to the pilots, 36 enemy bombers from Air Attack Force #1 of Japan's 24th Air Flotilla were flying towards Wake at an altitude one-half mile below the Wildcats.

At about noon, all hell broke loose. The Japanese bombers, flying from a base 720 miles to the south at Kwajalein, came over Wake in "V" formations and immediately headed for the airfield. Eight of the F4Fs, parked at 100-foot intervals at the airfield, were caught on the ground. Hit with 100-pound bombs and 20mm bullets, seven planes were destroyed and the eighth severely damaged. Twenty-three squadron members were killed, including pilots Graves and Holden. It was a devasting blow to VMF-211.

The bombers hit both Camp 1 and Camp 2, and they destroyed the Pan Am facilities. Killed in the attack were 10 Chamorro employees of Pan Am. The airline's "Clipper," parked at the dock, escaped with a few bullet holes, but aviation fuel drums and storage tanks were destroyed, and an additional 55 civilians killed.

During the raid, the defense force managed to get its anti-aircraft guns into action, but, due to the complete surprise with which the bombers attacked, the anti-aircraft fire was rendered largely ineffective. With no air raid warning system, and with the surf pounding loudly against the shore, aircraft could not be heard until they were over the island.

The raid ended as quickly as it began. It was an inauspicious way for the Wake Islanders to begin the war—the island suffered heavy damage, and no enemy planes had been downed. Though they didn't know it, the Wake Islanders would have another 15 days of fighting to avenge that first attack.

The destruction and loss of life was enormous, but in the next few days the Wake Islanders worked feverishly to repair the damage and strengthen their defenses. The Marines worked on coastal defenses, repaired communications and in general strengthened their posture.

While the Pan Am "Clipper" had taken off for Hawaii an hour after the attack with passengers and Pan Am personnel, hundreds of other civilians remained on the island. Dan Teters and many of his civilian construction workers pitched in to do what they could for the island's defense.

Rear Adm. Winfield Scott Cunningham

Commander of the entire American garrison at Wake Island, Cunningham had a long and distinguished career in the U.S. Navy.

Born in Wisconsin, he entered the U.S. Naval Academy in 1916 when he was 16 years old. After graduating in 1919, he saw extended sea duty in the Near and Far East. Following his first flight in a Navy plane at Pearl Harbor, he applied in 1924 for naval aviation training and received his wings the next year.

Cunningham then served as an aviator for many years, a career which included qualified landings on the Navy's first aircraft carrier, the *Langley*. In 1940, he was named navigator of the seaplane tender *USS Wright*, and in November 1941 he was assigned to temporary duty on Wake as commander of the naval air station then under construction on the island.

Cmdr. Cunningham spent 44 months in Japanese POW camps—including stints in solitary confinement as punishment for two escape attempts. He returned to the United States in 1945, was promoted to captain, and served in Pensacola and commanded a seaplane tender. On his final assignment he commanded the Naval Air Technical Training Center at Memphis, Tenn., where he retired as a rear admiral in 1950.

Cunningham and his wife of 57 years, Louise, live in Memphis. Both Cunningham and his wife spent many years trying to set the record straight in regard to his role in the Wake Island battle. Cunningham's book outlining his case, *Wake Island Command*, was published in 1961.

Lt. W.S. Cunningham in 1928.

NA (#80-G-465546)

Revetments were dug to protect the remaining F4Fs and dugouts and foxholes constructed for protection against air raids. Civilian and military doctors joined forces, setting up a hospital in the civilian facilities that was used throughout the battle.

At the airfield, Lt. John Kinney and his ground crew worked miracles repairing and servicing the remaining Wildcats, and by Dec. 9 at least four planes were in flying condition despite repeated raids by the Japanese. The garrison also mined the airfield as a precaution against enemy landings and set up a defense around the field.

The civilians not helping with defense or engaged in other construction projects were scattered in the brush throughout the three islets. Yet other members of Dan Teters' civilian crew took over the feeding of both civilian and military personnel—a difficult task at best. Meanwhile, the Wake Islanders hoped for additional troops to ward off the Japanese attackers, and in Pearl Harbor a relief task force was being prepared for the job.

As the islanders worked frantically on the island's defenses, they also had to face repeated Japanese attacks. The three days after the initial attack brought intense, but predictable, air raids by Japanese bombers, which went after the remaining aircraft facilities as well as the anti-aircraft and coastal

USS Triton (SS-201) at Dutch Harbor, Alaska, 1942. Patrolling south of Wake on December 10 she fired four torpedoes at one of the Japanese task force ships causing some damage. This was the first torpedo attack made by a Pacific Fleet submarine in World War II.   Pacific Submarine Museum, Pearl Harbor, Hawaii

The Yubari, I.J.N., a Japanese light cruiser that was damaged in the Dec. 11 attack and also participated in the Dec. 23 attack.   USN (#NH 82098)

The Tenryu, I.J.N., was damaged during the abortive Japanese landing on Dec. 11 when Wildcats put her torpedo battery out of action. She returned to Wake two weeks later. On Dec. 18, 1942, she was sunk by a submarine in the Bismarck Sea.   USMC Heinl Collection

defenses. While doing some damage, the raids were mostly ineffective, and the raid of Dec. 10 on Wilkes netted the Japanese nothing.

The air raids were intended to soften up Wake's defenses for a forced landing on its beaches. Adm. Inouye, commander of the Imperial Japanese 4th Fleet at Truk, had decided to take the island on Dec. 11. Commander of the operation would be Rear Adm. Kajioka, who flew his flag from the light cruiser *Yubari*. He had at his disposal three older light cruisers, the *Yubari*, *Tatsuta* and *Tenryu*; six old destroyers, the *Oite*, *Hayate*, *Mutsuki*, *Kisaragi*, *Mochizuki* and *Yayoi*; two patrol boats; and the medium transports *Kongo Maru* and *Konryu Maru*. The force also included 450 men of the Special Naval Landing Force who were to storm Wake's beaches.

Kajioka's chief of staff, Capt. Tudashi Koyama has described the landing plan as follows.

> In general, the plan was to have 150 men land on Wilkes Island and the balance, 300 men, on the south side of Wake Island to capture the airfield. The northeast coast was unsuitable for amphibious landings; also we didn't think this was too favorable a place due to the defenses. The alternative landing plan was that in the event of bad winds on the south side of the island we would land on the northeast and north coast. We expected to have a rough time and that we would have difficulty with a landing force of only 450 men. It was at the beginning of the war; we couldn't mass as many men as we considered necessary, and it was planned in an emergency to use the crews of the destroyers to storm the beach.

As it turned out, the Japanese did have a very rough time of it. At 0300 on Dec. 11, the Japanese force lay off Wake, ready to make its move. No sign of activity emerged from the darkness of the island. The force approached the island on a northwesterly course, with winds and rough seas making it very difficult for the troops to disembark into small boats for the beach assault.

The Marines had spotted the ships through the darkness and a command went out to hold fire until the Japanese had sailed closer. Since some of the shore batteries were without adequate range and direction finders and were lacking enough personnel, surprise was the Americans' best weapon against the landing force. Four Wildcats still were operational, but they were ordered to remain on the ground until the shore batteries commenced firing.

By 0500 the *Yubari* was 8,000 yards off Peacock Point. She turned westward and began a barrage broadside against Wake's south shore, with the force's other two cruisers following suit. An hour later, the *Yubari* was between 4,000 yards and 6,000 yards off Battery A (Peacock Point) when the battery was ordered to open fire. The salvos were on target and the *Yubari* was hit. She started to steam away, while one of the protecting destroyers began to lay a smoke

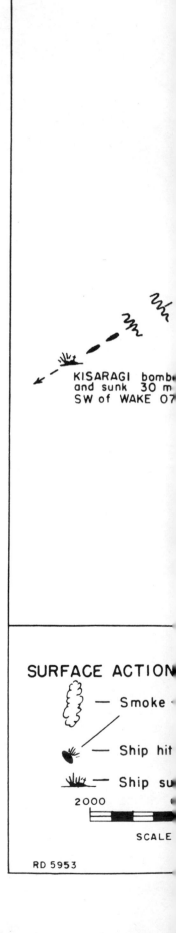

KISARAGI bomb and sunk 30 m SW of WAKE 07

SURFACE ACTION

— Smoke

— Ship hit

— Ship su

2000

SCALE

RD 5953

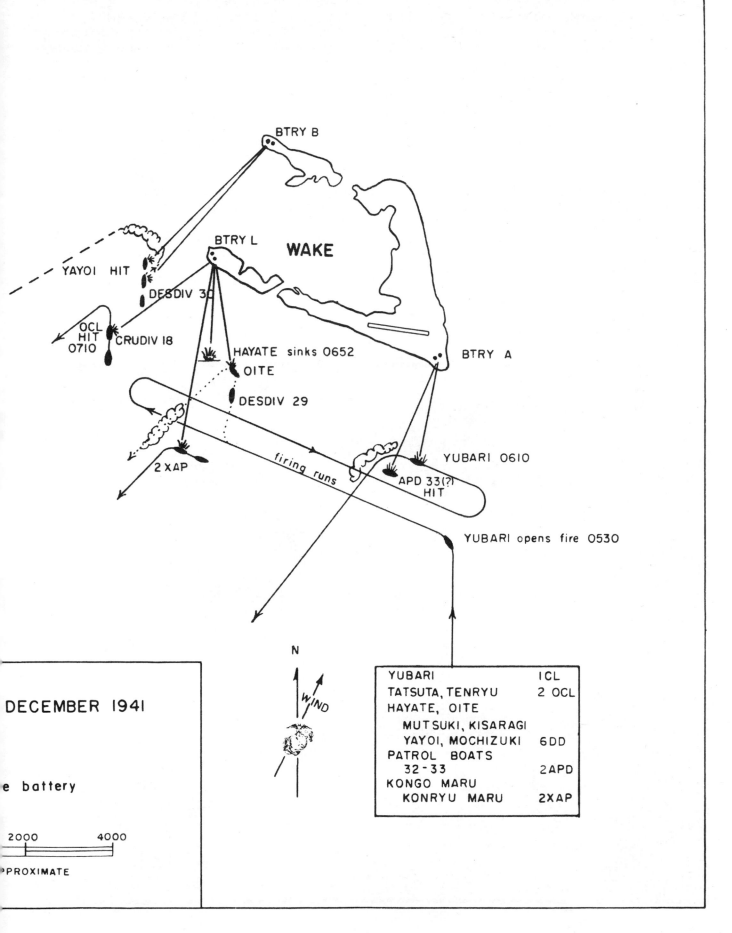

BTRY B

BTRY L

WAKE

YAYOI HIT

DESDIV 30

OCL
HIT
0710   CRUDIV 18

HAYATE sinks 0652

OITE

DESDIV 29

BTRY A

firing runs

2 XAP

YUBARI 0610

APD 33(?)
HIT

YUBARI opens fire 0530

DECEMBER 1941

e battery

2000   4000

PROXIMATE

N

WIND

YUBARI	ICL
TATSUTA, TENRYU	2 OCL
HAYATE, OITE	
MUTSUKI, KISARAGI	
YAYOI, MOCHIZUKI	6 DD
PATROL BOATS	
32-33	2 APD
KONGO MARU	
KONRYU MARU	2 XAP

screen. That destroyer also was hit.

On Wilkes, Battery L had even better luck. Three destroyers, two transports and the cruisers *Tatsuta* and *Tenryu* were about 4,000 yards off the island when the battery opened up and scored a direct hit on the destroyer *Hayate.* The ship exploded violently and sunk with all hands. Battery L also scored hits on the destroyer *Oite,* one of the transports and one cruiser.

Battery B on Peale also tasted action. The battery's salvos hit the destroyer *Yayoi* at its stern and the ship retired behind a smoke screen.

With the rough weather and many of the force's ships damaged or sunk, the Japanese commander decided to turn back to Kwajalein without attempting a landing. The retreat was not an easy one, however. By this time, VMF-211's planes were in the air, and they proceeded to attack the retreating task force,

which was without air cover. The *Tenryu* and *Tatsuta* were hit and the transport *Kongo Maru* and possibly a patrol boat also took hits. The biggest score of the day was the sinking of the destroyer *Kisaragi,* possibly by VMF-211's Capt. Elrod.

The Japanese inflicted relatively light damage on the Americans. Elrod's plane crash-landed at the airfield and was a total wreck. The shore batteries suffered some irreparable damage, but only four Marines were wounded. In return, the Americans had exacted a heavy toll from the enemy for its attempted landing: three cruisers damaged, two destroyers and possibly one patrol boat sunk, one transport damaged and possibly over 700 men lost from the ships.

It was a great day for the Wake Islanders, but it was only a prelude to another 12 days of harrassment and battle.

Notes on the Sinking Of a Japanese Cruiser Off Wake by VMF-211

Following is Lt. Col. Paul Putnam's account of the sinking of a Japanese light cruiser off Wake Island at 0530 on Dec. 11, 1941. Putnam, the commanding officer of VMF-211 while it was on Wake, gave the account to Lt. Edna Loftus Smith, MCWR, on Oct. 19, 1945, after he had been released from an enemy POW camp in Japan.

0300 11 December. The beach lookout reported a Japanese surface force off Wake. One large ship appeared to be a carrier. The squadron took off well before daylight; in preparation to attack a carrier they went up to 20,000' and maintained that altitude until well after daylight. There were four planes which joined in the surface fight. The ships were bombarding the island and two batteries were answering them. Our attack was delayed by the sudden formation of a thin but solid cloud layer at 1,000 feet. The cloud layer dispersed after an hour or

so almost as suddenly as it formed. Afterwards we operated under ideal conditions.

As Col. Putnam saw it, the enemy force consisted of 1 light cruiser, 9 destroyers and 2 merchant ships.* The light cruiser was an old and small model. The first attack by VMF-211 was executed by two plane sections but thereafter each plane returned to the beach, rearmed and refueled as rapidly as possible and attacked individually.

A bomb dropped by Elrod apparently inflicted the fatal damage on the cruiser. "I saw the bomb drop and the appearance of the explosion gave every indication that it has in some manner penetrated the interior of the ship. The ship almost immediately lost way and lay dead in the water for a good half hour. It could be seen unmistakably that she was afire internally. She evidently got under way again slowly and followed the retiring destroyers to the southward. On my last sortie as I was approaching this light cruiser at a point some thirty miles south of the island and while I was looking directly at her she just changed from a ship to a ball of flame and was sunk within a matter of seconds."

---

* 10 Dec. 41 Pearl Harbor Time.

The Battle
Second Phase: Dec. 12-23, 1941

The 11 days after the abortive Japanese landing of Dec. 11 can be summed up as a period of increased enemy air activity interspersed with stretches of quiet and apprehension. It all ended, however, on Dec. 23 after the Japanese landed on Wake Island.

During the previous 11 days enemy bombers, and eventually enemy fighters, flew sorties over Wake at any hour of the day or night. And during these 11 days, the Wake Islanders simply did not have much to do except wait for the next raid and hope for the relief force to show up.

Most of the feasible defensive work had been completed. Furthermore, it was impossible for the civilians to continue their construction work. The island had no air-warning system, and the workers could not operate heavy machinery for fear its noise would block out the sound of approaching enemy planes.

VMF-211's ground crewmen, however, had their hands full. Both military and civilian personnel worked to keep the few remaining Wildcats in the air, while the pilots of VMF-211, along with the anti-aircraft guns, were chalking up an impressive score against enemy bombers.

By this time, the enemy was not finding much left to bomb on Wake except anti-aircraft batteries and what remained of the airfield. But every hit on one of the guns weakened the island's defenses.

Whenever the enemy determined an anti-aircraft gun's location, the battery had to be moved—a difficult task considering that the guns weighed many tons. Usually the job took an entire night, and was handled by both Marines and civilians.

Meanwhile, the Japanese invasion force was not about to give up. It had been defeated once, and had limped back to Kwajalein on Dec. 13, but the second invasion would be different. Adm. Kajioka was again given the command. Japanese planners added to the invasion force four replacement destroyers—the *Tusagaru*, *Asanagi*, *Yunagi*, and *Oboro*—a mine layer, two transports, a floatplane tender and several submarines. The cruisers that had been damaged in the first invasion attempt were repaired and again took places in the force.

Japanese planners also intended to provide an adequate landing force for the second invasion attempt. The Maizuru 2nd Special Landing Force was brought from Saipan, bringing the total landing force to about 1,000 men, along with a 500-man reserve force. A tactical change was made for the second attempt—there would be no pre-invasion bombardment to warn the Wake Islanders of the fleet's approach. According to the plan, the force would land in the dark and the two transports and patrol boats would be run aground on the south shore of Wake near the airstrip. Six landing barges would ground themselves elsewhere along the south shores of Wake and Wilkes.

To ensure the invasion's success, a Japanese carrier group was directed towards Wake. Made up of the carriers *Soryu* and *Hiryu* plus cruisers, the group, which was en route to Japan from the Pearl Harbor attack, would provide air strikes and would guard against any American surface intervention from the north and west. Japanese Cruiser Division 6 would provide cover to the south and east of Wake.

While the Japanese made their invasion plans, the Wake Islanders took whatever comfort they could from various bits of good news. A submarine was sunk on Dec. 12 by VMF-211's Lt. Kliewer. It was thought that this sub had been sending radio homing signals to guide enemy bombers towards Wake.

On Dec. 13, the Japanese did not execute an air raid on Wake, the first day of quiet in five days, nor

For sixteen days the Japs pounded away at the rock from the air and sea. The Nips were thrown for quite a loss all the way. At lower right is a Japs eye view of our little island.

Devereux's Marine command post during the battle was in this magazine, located near the airfield.

did Dec. 18 bring an air raid. Dec. 20 was a joyful day for the Wake Islanders—a Navy PBY flew in at 1530 from Pearl Harbor with news that a relief force was on its way. The force was to evacuate most of the civilians and bring additional Marines and planes.

The PBY left for Hawaii early the next morning, loaded with mail and carrying Maj. Walter Bayler. Bayler had been sent to Wake in November on a temporary assignment to establish communications for the air squadron. He would be the last man off Wake before its surrender and he would be the first American to set foot again on the island in 1945.

On Dec. 21, the day of the PBY's departure, the battle took a decided turn for the worse. Twenty-nine Japanese attack bombers flew over the island, and for the first time they were protected by Japanese fighter planes. The presence of the 18 fighters indicated that enemy carriers were in the vicinity of Wake. Other ships undoubtedly would be with it.

VMF-211 was down to two planes and now the numbers would be overwhelmingly against them. By the end of the next day, the squadron would be without any serviceable Wildcats at all.

Capt. Freuler and Lt. Davidson took off on Dec. 22 in the remaining two Wildcats to oppose 39 enemy bombers and fighters. They shot down several Japanese planes before Davidson disappeared and Freuler, his plane damaged when an enemy plane exploded nearby, crash-landed on the island. No longer having any planes in the squadron, Maj. Putnam placed his remaining men as infantry at the disposal of Maj. Devereux. These men had fought hard for 15 days and, along with the anti-aircraft crews, had accounted for 21 enemy planes destroyed and approximately 50 enemy planes damaged—an impressive

number considering the equipment they had to work with.

By this time, the end was near, although Wake's defenders did not know it. As far as they knew, the relief force was coming at any time. They also knew that with enemy carriers in the area, the relief force had better come soon.

The Anti-Aircraft Artillery Batteries on Wake were probably the best in the Marine Corps at that point in time (1941). Many of the non-commissioned officers had been with AAA since the first 3-inch guns and equipment was unpacked at Quantico, Va., in the summer of 1937. They had progressed into the 2nd Battalion 15th Marines and on into the First Defense Battalion.

The AAA fire on Wake was so effective that the Japanese bombers soon developed a healthy respect for the "sky gunners" and came in higher and higher each day trying to avoid the flack. By 22 December the bombers were completely above the range of the 21 second mechanical time fuzes on the AA projectiles. This caused the bombing to be less effective.

Enemy documents captured on 24 December 1943 at Tarawa stated that from December 8-23, 1941, over 55 aircraft returned to base damaged and some with men killed aboard the aircraft. In addition to the 55 aircraft damaged, the Japanese report for December 8 listed "several planes damaged, 1 petty officer killed by shell fire." Although the fighters (F4Fs) and AAA shot down a combined 21 Japanese aircraft most of the damaged aircraft was due to the accurate AAA fire. *

*Joint Intelligence Center, Pacific Ocean Areas Item Number 4986 (Translation of Captured Japanese Document, JICPOA date 25 February 1944-Serial ADM-250829). From an interview with CW04 Charles A. Holmes, USMC (Retired) on August 2, 1984.

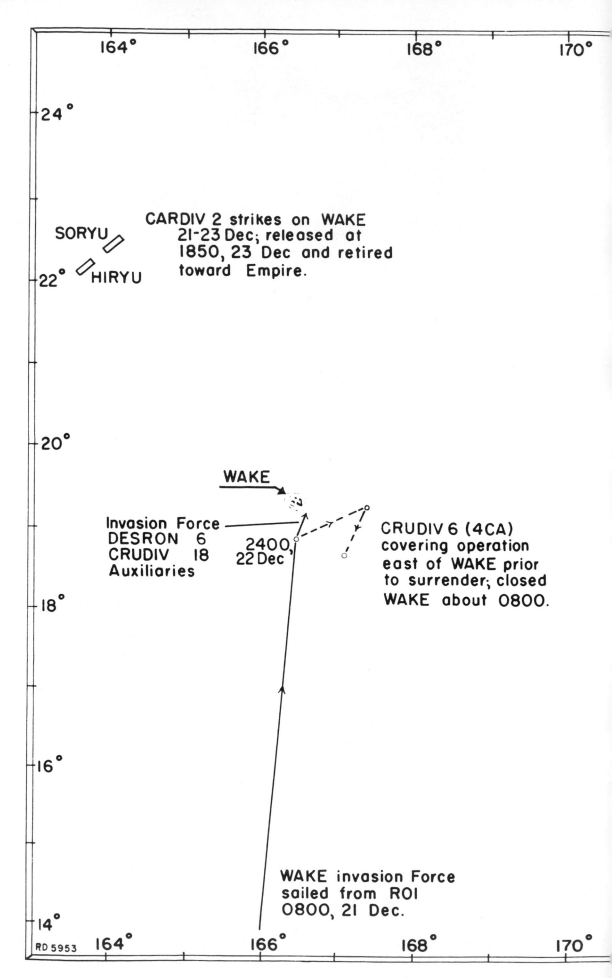

SORYU

HIRYU

CARDIV 2 strikes on WAKE
21-23 Dec; released at
1850, 23 Dec and retired
toward Empire.

WAKE

Invasion Force
DESRON 6
CRUDIV 18
Auxiliaries

2400,
22 Dec

CRUDIV 6 (4CA)
covering operation
east of WAKE prior
to surrender; closed
WAKE about 0800.

WAKE invasion Force
sailed from ROI
0800, 21 Dec.

RD 5953

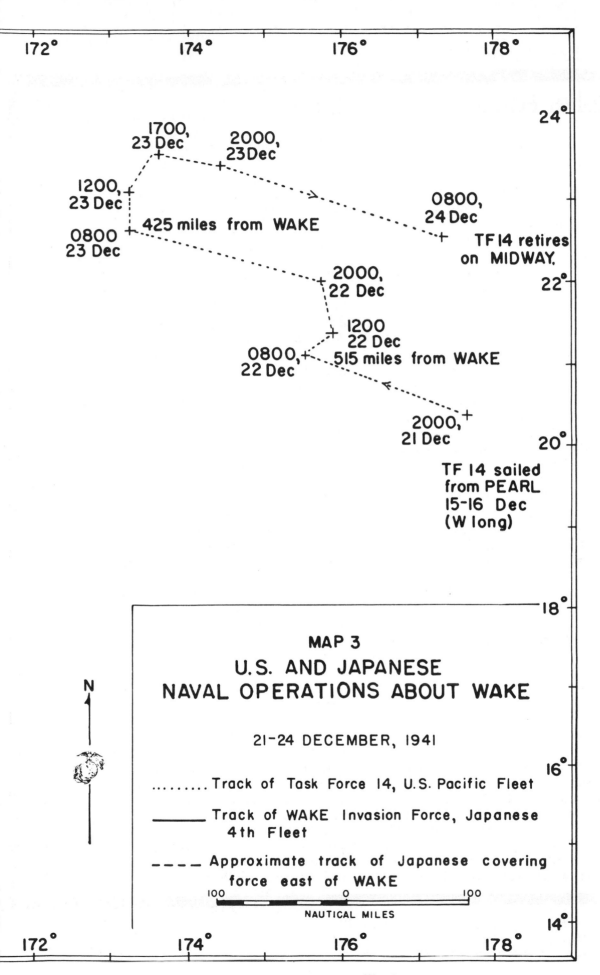

172°   174°   176°   178°

24°

1700,
23 Dec   2000,
     23Dec

1200,
23 Dec   0800,
24 Dec

0800   425 miles from WAKE
23 Dec   TF14 retires
on MIDWAY.

22°

2000,
22 Dec

1200
22 Dec

0800,   515 miles from WAKE
22 Dec

2000,
21 Dec

20°

TF 14 sailed
from PEARL
15-16 Dec
(W long)

18°

MAP 3

**U.S. AND JAPANESE
NAVAL OPERATIONS ABOUT WAKE**

21-24 DECEMBER, 1941

N

16°

.... Track of Task Force 14, U.S. Pacific Fleet

———— Track of WAKE Invasion Force, Japanese
         4th Fleet

– – – Approximate track of Japanese covering
         force east of WAKE

100   0   100

NAUTICAL MILES

14°

172°   174°   176°   178°

Relief Force

After continuous pounding by enemy forces, the Wake Islanders desperately needed help. Their only hope was a relief force from Hawaii.

The relief force grew out of a plan that was formulated in Pearl Harbor during the chaotic aftermath of the Dec. 7 attack. Put together by Adm. Husband Kimmel and his staff, the plan would be Kimmel's last act before he was removed from command on Dec. 17, 1941.

Preparations for the Wake relief force quickly got under way. By Dec. 10, the command on Oahu had mustered whatever it could spare in the way of supplies and reinforcements, including a contingent from the 4th Marine Defense Battalion.

The plan was built around the three remaining carriers on duty in the Pacific area. The *USS Lexington* would take Task Force 11, under the command of Vice Adm. Wilson Brown, close to the Marshall Islands, and there would execute a diversionary raid on Jaluit. The *USS Enterprise* and Task Force 8, under the command of Vice Adm. William F. Halsey, would operate to the west of Johnston Island and would cover the approaches to Hawaii and possibly cover the main relief force as well.

The actual relief trip to Wake would be made by the carrier *USS Saratoga* and Task Force 14, under the command of Rear Adm. Frank Jack Fletcher.

The *Saratoga*, which was still off the West Coast of the United States, had on board VMF-221, a Marine fighter squadron consisting of 18 Brewster Buffalos that were to reinforce VMF-211 on Wake. The task force also included Destroyer Squadron 4 and the three remaining cruisers of Adm. Jack Fletcher's Cruiser Division 6—the *USS Astoria*, the *USS Minneapolis* and the *USS San Francisco*. In addition, the force included the fleet oiler, *USS Neches*, and the seaplane tender *USS Tangier*, which according to the plan was to play a central role in the relief effort.

Although he had no experience with carriers, Fletcher, the senior officer, was named the commander of the entire relief task force by Adm. Kimmel.

According to the relief plan, the *Tangier* would make a fast run to Wake, anchor to buoys in the roadstead off Wilkes, unload supplies and troops and take on the wounded. Meanwhile, VMF-221 would fly off the *Saratoga*, which would be lying a safe distance from the island. The fighters would remain on Wake to reinforce the island's air defenses.

Despite the promptness of the preparations, the actual launching of the three task forces was delayed by a number of problems. Part of the delay resulted from the change in command at Pearl Harbor from Adm. Kimmel to his temporary successor, Vice Adm. W.S. Pye. The departure also was delayed by the refueling of the carriers and the late arrival in Pearl Harbor of the *Saratoga*, which was making its way west from the United States. In addition, the entire operation was hampered by faulty intelligence, in particular the unknown location of enemy carriers that were believed to be in the vicinity of Wake, having stopped near the island on their return from the Pearl Harbor attack.

The three task forces left Pearl Harbor at different times between Dec. 14 and Dec. 16, but neither of the two support task forces fulfilled its original mission, largely because CINCPAC in Pearl Harbor became increasingly concerned that some of the carriers would be lost..

This left the main relief force basically on its own. The *Saratoga* was sailing into an area that, according to rumor and intelligence, was infested with enemy forces. Meanwhile, the detachment on Wake braced for a final enemy assault.

More problems developed for the relief force as it steamed towards Wake. Fletcher's destroyers were having fueling troubles and CINCPAC was still worried about losing a carrier. Due to CINCPAC's indecision and due to the fueling troubles, the relief force was called back to Pearl on Dec. 23. At the time the relief force was only 425 miles from Wake, and the island's surrender was just hours away.

The cancellation of the relief mission came as a big disappointment to the task force's servicemen, especially the Marines aboard the *Tangier*, who were eager to help their comrades on Wake.

Whether the relief force could have saved the garrison and whether all the ships would have survived is a matter of conjecture. After the war, however, it was learned that the *Soryu* and the *Hiryu* were stationed 250 miles northwest of Wake at the time of the relief force's effort. This distance was too great for the carriers to menace the incoming task force.

But it might not have made any difference if the Japanese carriers' positions had been known. Even before it called back the relief force, the Navy had actually written off Wake Island as lost to the enemy.

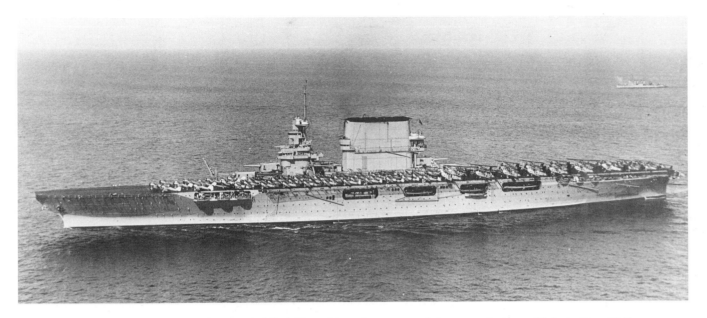

USS Saratoga *(CV-3), the ship that led Task Force 14 on the unsuccessful rescue mission to Wake in Dec. 1941.*
USN (#NH 75885)

USS Minneapolis *(CA-36).*
NA (#80-G-425607)

USS Astoria *(CA-34).*
NA (#19-N-25347)

USS San Francisco *(CA-38)*.
NA (#19-N-30283)

USS Neches *(AO-5), fleet oiler.*
NA (#80-G-456386)

USS Tangier *(AV-8), converted from a seaplane tender to a troop transport.* NA (#19-N-25362)

The relief force never arrived, but the Japanese invasion force did. In the early-morning darkness of Dec. 23, Japanese landing craft beached at Wake and Wilkes. Only about 200 Marines were available to man the beach defenses; the remainder of the Marines, plus some civilians, were manning the 3" and 5" guns. The Wake Islanders had spotted the landing craft when they were a short distance offshore, but the defenders were spread too thinly to control all points on the three islets.

Wilkes was hit first with 100 men of the Takano Company.* As the Japanese came ashore, the defenders momentarily turned a searchlight on them, and then the 70 Marines that were defending the Wilkes beach under Capt. Wesley Platt let loose with everything they had. But the Japanese drove back the defenders. Communications were lost with Devereux's command post on Wake, as well as among the Wilkes Marines themselves.

At about the same time, on the south shore of Wake, two patrol boats beached and unloaded the Uchida and Itaya companies. Only one 3" gun was in the vicinity of the landing and it was unmanned. Lt. Robert Hanna and four others raced to the gun and fired point blank at the disembarking enemy. The gun's fire was devastating, but there were just too many invaders, and soon Hanna's crew, in addition to 27 men of Putnam's command, were fighting hand-to-hand with the enemy. The defenders, taking casualties, were slowly squeezed into small pockets.

At the airfield on Wake, Lt. Kliewer and four Marines were at the western end of the field and were ordered to set off dynamite charges if the enemy advanced towards them. Unfortunately, the wires from the generator to the charges had shorted out and the charges could not be set off as the enemy approached.

At Camp 1 on Wake, Devereux's mobile reserve, headed by Lt. Art Poindexter, set up a defense perimeter around the camp. The 20 Marines and 14 civilians were soon joined by others. Earlier, Poindexter and a few men had raced towards the beach, throwing hand grenades at the enemy invaders.

As the battle raged all over Wake islet, the defenders were pushed into smaller and smaller pockets. From his command post, Devereux was losing touch with his men. At 0500 Capt. Cunningham, in his own command post, sent the message to Pearl Harbor—"Enemy on island. Issue in doubt."

The final reserve, Capt. Bryghte Godbold's 60 men from Peale, which had not been invaded, were ordered to Wake to bolster the defensive lines. On Wilkes, Platt's men staged a counterattack and eventually wiped out the entire 100-man Japanese landing party at the cost of nine Marines and two civilians. At Wake's Camp 1, Poindexter's group was still holding out and actually counterattacking in spots.

Nevertheless, by sunup it was clear that the enemy controlled Wake islet. Over 1,000 Japanese were ashore, the sea was full of enemy ships (27 total), and the enemy completely controlled the air.

There was no alternative other than a complete surrender of the atoll. Devereux called Cunningham to get permission to surrender. Gunner John Hamas, a 20-year Marine and a former lieutenant in the Czechoslovakian army, walked in to Devereux's command post to get orders and was told to fix a white flag and pass the word to cease fire.

Hiryu, the Japanese aircraft carrier that along with the Soryu *participated in the second invasion of Wake Island on Dec. 23. Both of these carriers had participated in the Pearl Harbor attack.*   USN (#NH 73063)

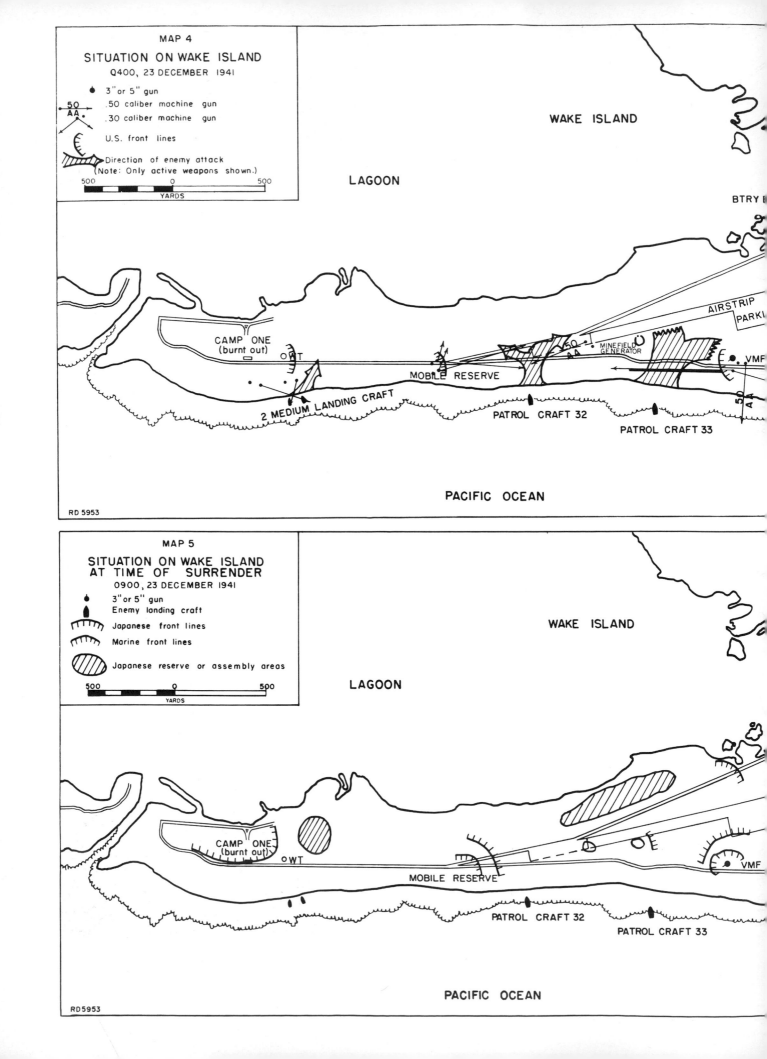

MAP 4

SITUATION ON WAKE ISLAND

0400, 23 DECEMBER 1941

- 3" or 5" gun
- .50 caliber machine gun
- .30 caliber machine gun
- U.S. front lines
- Direction of enemy attack

(Note: Only active weapons shown.)

500   0   500
YARDS

WAKE ISLAND

LAGOON

BTRY

AIRSTRIP

PARKI

CAMP ONE
(burnt out)

WT

MOBILE RESERVE

MINEFIELD
GENERATOR

50
AA

VMF

50
AA

2 MEDIUM LANDING CRAFT

PATROL CRAFT 32

PATROL CRAFT 33

PACIFIC OCEAN

RD 5953

MAP 5

**SITUATION ON WAKE ISLAND
AT TIME OF SURRENDER**

0900, 23 DECEMBER 1941

- 3" or 5" gun
- Enemy landing craft
- Japanese front lines
- Marine front lines
- Japanese reserve or assembly areas

500   0   500
YARDS

WAKE ISLAND

LAGOON

CAMP ONE
(burnt out)

WT

MOBILE RESERVE

VMF

PATROL CRAFT 32

PATROL CRAFT 33

PACIFIC OCEAN

RD 5953

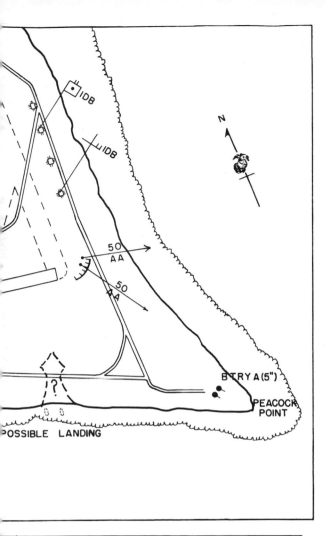

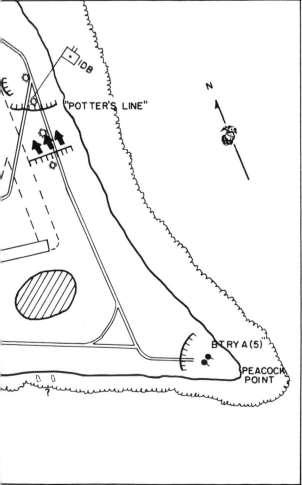

It would take six hours to stop the fighting. Some of the Marines could not believe they had to surrender—it simply was not in their training. When they were finally convinced, the Marines destroyed their weapons and came out of the bush. Cunningham left his command post in the bush, went to the cottage he had occupied before the war had broken out, shaved, put on a clean blue uniform, and drove to the surrender.

The Japanese rounded up all the civilians and enlisted men and marched them to the airfield. There the prisoners were stripped to their shoes and bound with wire. They spent two days on the field, with no food and little water. The officers were kept in the island's remaining cottages.

When Devereux heard of the treatment the prisoners were receiving at the airfield, he protested to the Japanese, and the Americans were finally moved to the remains of Camp 2. Later, the prisoners were put to work cleaning up the battle's debris, and most of them were evacuated from the island on Jan. 12, 1942.

Wake had been a costly battle for the Japanese. In the 16 days of fighting, a total of 820 Japanese were killed, and 333 wounded.** American casualties totaled 120 killed, 49 wounded and two missing.

---

* The Japanese companies were named for their company commanders.
** These figures include air, naval and ground casualties.

2nd Lt. Arthur A. Poindexter, commander of Devereux's mobile reserve. A pre-war photo.   Stegmaier Collection

Close-up views of a diorama depicting the Japanese invasion of Wake Island on Dec. 23, 1941. It was built by students of Gilbert Junior High School, Gilbert, Ariz., and is housed in the Marine Corps Air Museum, Quantico, Va.

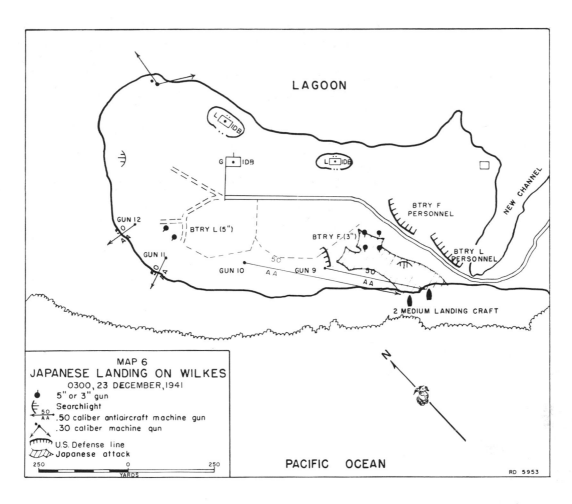

MAP 6
JAPANESE LANDING ON WILKES
0300, 23 DECEMBER, 1941

● 5" or 3" gun
€ 50 Searchlight
— 50 AA .50 caliber antiaircraft machine gun
⋀ .30 caliber machine gun

⏜⏜⏜ U.S. Defense line
⟋⟋ Japanese attack

250   0   250
YARDS

LAGOON

L • IDB
G • IDB
L • IDB

NEW CHANNEL

BTRY F PERSONNEL

GUN 12
BTRY L (5")
GUN 11
BTRY F (3")
BTRY L PERSONNEL
GUN 10
GUN 9
2 MEDIUM LANDING CRAFT

N

PACIFIC OCEAN

RD 5953

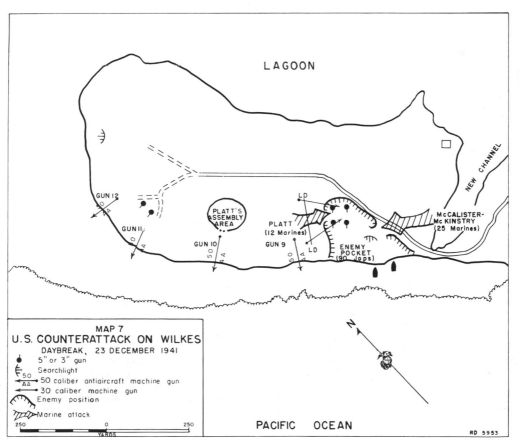

MAP 7
U.S. COUNTERATTACK ON WILKES
DAYBREAK, 23 DECEMBER 1941

● 5" or 3" gun
€ 50 Searchlight
— 50 AA 50 caliber antiaircraft machine gun
← 30 caliber machine gun
⏜⏜⏜ Enemy position
⟋⟋ Marine attack

250   0   250
YARDS

LAGOON

NEW CHANNEL

GUN 12
GUN 11
PLATT'S ASSEMBLY AREA
GUN 10
GUN 9
PLATT (12 Marines)
LD
LD
ENEMY POCKET (90 Japs)
McCALISTER-McKINSTRY (25 Marines)

N

PACIFIC OCEAN

RD 5953

-45-

Painting of the Dec. 23 battle by Albert Henning.

USMC (#307142)

A rare Japanese aerial photo of Wake Island before the island was occupied.

Author's Collection

Remains of fuel storage tanks near the Marine camp. Photo taken after the Japanese occupation.   NA (#80-G-413518)

A war-time Japanese painting by Matsuzaka Yasu represents the conquest of Wake Island on Dec. 23, 1941.
USA (#SC 301066)

Japanese victors examine a covered revetment that protected one of the Wildcat fighters. The large hill in the background is actually a mound of sand that was piled up when the revetment was dug. Photo from a Japanese picture book.

ウエーキ島を占領

開戦と共に、わが航空部隊が猛爆のウエーキ島めざし二十二日夜半、特型駆逐艦隊は、荒れ狂ふ南海の怒濤を冒して果敢な敵前上陸を敢行し翌日これを占領、その名も大島島と改称す。

Aerial photo, taken from an attacking Japanese plane, of the civilian construction workers' barracks on Wake. This was the living area for the approximately 1,200 civilians working on the island. Photo from a Japanese picture book.

A Japanese photo of a wrecked F4F-3 Wildcat on Wake after the island's capture. NA (#80-G-413519)

The graveyard for planes of VMF-211, the fighter squadron that fought in the defense of Wake. The photo originally appeared in a Japanese picture book. USMC (#315173)

VMF-211 Wildcats that were destroyed on Wake by Japanese bombers. Author's Collection

Japanese troops pay homage to a memorial erected to unit commander Uchida, who was killed in the Japanese landing on Wake on Dec. 23, 1941. Photo from a Japanese picture book.   USMC (#315175)

Japanese flag raising on Wake Island. Photo from a Japanese picture book.
USMC (#315169)

A Japanese aviator tells his comrades about his flying adventures over Wake in December 1941. Photo from a Japanese picture book.
USMC (#315178)

THE IDAHO DAILY STATESMAN

Published Every Day—No. 135   ESTABLISHED 1864   Boise, Idaho, Monday Morning, December 29, 1941   ASSOCIATED PRESS DAY AND NIGHT LEASED WIRES   Price Five Cents

U. S. Reveals Heroism at Wake

Roosevelt and Navy Pledge Help for Embattled Philippines

Senator Says U. S. Navy Lists 14 Civilians Killed at Wake

WASHINGTON (AP)—Senator McCarran (D-Nev.) said Sunday night that the Navy listed 14 fatalities among about 1000 civilian construction workers on Wake island.

One of those killed was Joe McDonald, Jr., of Reno, an engineer and the son of the editor of the Nevada State Journal.

McCarran said that McDonald was the only Nevadan among those killed and that he did not make note of the names of the other 13 when he inspected the casualty list at the Navy department Saturday. Reporters seeking to obtain the names direct from the Navy were told by officers that the list was "not available."

The families of Fritz Schaefer, 22, Nampa, Idaho, and Louis A. Adamson, 26, Twin Falls, were notified last week the two men were killed during the attacks on Wake.

Many hundreds of Idaho men were employed on Wake and other Pacific outposts, but no other casualties have been announced.

News of War At a Glance

By the Associated Press

Japanese bomb undefended Manila for second consecutive day as leaders in Tokio claim Gen. Douglas MacArthur's proclamation of city as open was "unilateral"; land fighting on Luzon decreases in intensity; Philippine defenders still have situation in hand on northern front; War department warns of new Japanese pressure to come as reinforcements land on Lingayen gulf.

ON HOME FRONT

President Roosevelt pledges Philippines their "freedom will be redeemed and their independence established and protected; Navy adds its assurance that fleet is following "an intensive and well-planned assistance to the defense of the Philippine islands.

WAR CONFERENCE

London and Moscow announces British Foreign Secretary Anthony Eden and Russian Premier Joseph Stalin have been in conference in Moscow for two weeks, keeping in touch with Roosevelt-Churchill parley in Washington; United States, Great Britain and Russia unite in a common military and diplomatic program aimed at final destruction of Hitlerism.

IN FAR EAST

Japanese parachute troops land on Sumatra on flank of Singapore defenses; Netherlands East Indies sources say battle against invaders still under way; British forces in Malaya begin fourth week of war and defense of Singapore with announcement imperial troops have driven back Japanese after inflicting heavy losses in Perak state.

Violent Assault Told in Release Of First Details

Opening Raid on Isle Kills 25; Many More Wounded; Defenders Fought Great Odds

By TOM YARBROUGH

HONOLULU (AP)—A moving narrative of the heroic 14-day defense of tiny Wake island, given out Sunday by the Navy, told how the defending Marines, with only four planes in action, shot down at least a dozen Japanese planes and knocked out of action five enemy warships—three destroyers, a cruiser and a submarine.

Not until Dec. 22 in its final dispatch did the sadly outnumbered and overwhelmed garrison of less than 400 Marines admit defeat. Even then it reported "the issue is in doubt."

The last report from the mid-Pacific defense outpost 2500 miles west of Honolulu said the enemy had gained a foothold and more ships and a transport were moving in.

A dramatic account, compiled from official dispatches which were sent while the battle raged, said:

"Official reports indicate that probably no military force in American history, not even the defenders of the Alamo, ever fought against greater odds nor with greater effect in view of those odds."

The account disclosed that "no fewer than 200 Japanese airplanes bombed and machine-gunned the tiny island's defenders," not including those which came over in the final attack. Their number is unknown.

The island had only 12 planes when the assault was launched—almost at the same time Pearl Harbor was attacked. Four of Wake island's planes were in the air when the enemy appeared "in a low glide from a cloud bank."

Seven of the planes on the ground were rendered a total loss. Only remnants were salvaged from the eighth. The date of the initial attack was Dec. 8 on Wake island because it lies west of the international dateline.

In the closing days of the siege, the defenders had only two planes. They finally were reduced to one against the relentless raiders, moving in with as many as 50 planes at one time and "pulverizing" the beaches.

In the first raid, 25 of the defenders were killed and more than that number wounded.

By "pattern bombing" the Japanese had heavily damaged "practically every installation" on the island by the evening of Dec. 17.

The first attack from surface ships came on the third day of the battle.

"As dawn broke enemy warships started pumping shells to the flat and virtually shelterless atoll. There is practically no natural cover against bombardment on Wake. Except for man-made construction, its surface is bare and inhospitable. As the enemy warships opened fire, their aircraft came over in waves."

The Navy's account added: "Terse official dispatches make no mention of the garrison's feelings."

The Contractors camp was well demolished. Shown above is the Contractors warehouse. Behind and to the left, can be seen the conveyor belts and gravel piles where many of the men were able to take shelter. At the extreme left lies the remnants of the garage and machine shop.

After our capture on Dec. 23, 1941, we were marched off to the airport. As we trudged along the beach road we could see Jap ships plying around our tiny atoll.

TO THE GLORY OF A SCAR SPANGLED BANNER

SUN SPOTS !

Propaganda cartoons published in many American newspapers after the battle and surrender of Wake. They were intended to remind the public of the heroic defense of the island.   USMC

THE WAKE OF HISTORY

"SEMPER FIDELIS"

USMC

The POW Experience

With the American surrender of Wake on the afternoon of Dec. 23, 1941, the issue was no longer in doubt. The agonizing battle had ended, and the American soldiers and civilian construction workers were taken prisoner, soon to be sent to POW camps in China.

While still on Wake Island, the prisoners were at first treated very badly, but soon tensions eased and the Americans received better food and living quarters.

Then began the long trip to the east. On Jan. 12, 1942, the *Nitta Maru,* a converted passenger ship, loaded approximately 1,200 Americans for a grueling 12-day voyage to China. As they boarded, some of the men were forced to run a gauntlet between two lines formed by the ship's crew, who applied kicks and blows to the prisoners.

The ship stopped at Japan, leaving 20 of the prisoners there, and then went on towards China. During that crossing, five randomly-selected Americans were beheaded at the command of Lt. Toshio Saito, head of the ship's guards. After the war, four of the guards who participated in the beheadings were found guilty and sentenced to many years of hard labor. Saito was never located.

The several hundred American prisoners left behind by the *Nitta Maru* were taken off Wake later in 1942, but the Japanese kept 98 other American civilians on the island. These men, who were retained to operate heavy equipment, were executed on Oct. 7, 1943, by order of the island's commander, Adm. Sakaibara, on the pretext that they had been in radio contact with U.S. naval forces. Sakaibara radioed a report to his superiors stating, "Riotous conduct among prisoners. Have executed them." For this action, Sakaibara was tried and sentenced to hang, which took place at Guam on June 18, 1947.

Another group of American prisoners, consisting of 20 wounded servicemen, had been left on Wake so their injuries could heal. They were sent to Japan in May 1942, and eventually interned at the Zentsuji POW camp.

The main group of prisoners, aboard the *Nitta Maru,* arrived at Shanghai on Jan. 24 and were taken to Woosung camp 12 miles north of the city. A former Japanese Army base, Woosung would be home to the Wake Islanders as well as Marines from the North China legation garrison, sailors from the *USS Wake* and some British prisoners. Conditions at the camp were poor; health and sanitary facilities were inadequate and over 1,500 prisoners were crowded into seven old wooden barracks.

Most of the Wake Island prisoners were transferred to Kiangwan War Prisoners Camp, four miles from Shanghai, on Dec. 5, 1942. Although the Kiangwan camp was not much different than Woosung, the prisoners there were forced into hard labor building a rifle range (the Mount Fuji project). This caused many men to become very ill, and some to die.

As their internment stretched into 1944 and early 1945, the prisoners became increasingly aware that the Japanese were losing the war. Bombing missions blasted enemy installations around Shanghai and American planes flew low over the camp.

In May 1945, the Wake Islanders again were transferred, this time 700 miles north to the Fengtai camp just outside Peking. They stayed only a month before they were moved to the port city of Fusan (now Pusan), Korea, and then, after a stay of a few days, shipped to the island of Hokkaido, Japan. On Hokkaido the prisoners were interned at a number of camps and put to work in the local coal mines.

About mid-September 1945, the prison camps were

liberated by the U.S. 1st Cavalry Division, thus ending 44 months of brutal captivity for the Wake Islanders.

No Wake Islanders escaped from the prison camps in China and Japan, although Cmdr. Cunningham and Dan Teters made two unsuccessful attempts. However, while the prisoners were being transferred to Peking by rail, Lt. John Kinney of VMF-211 and four other prisoners successfully escaped from a moving train on May 10, 1945, reaching American forces 44 days later.

In total, the Japanese took 1,462 Americans from Wake to POW camps in China and Japan. Of these, 231 died in camp, on board ship, or while escaping.* Another 98 Americans were executed on Wake.

*Information from Packet #10, *The Japanese Story*, of the American Ex-POW Inc., National Medical Research Committee, 1979.

As cattle herded for slaughter, we were brought to the airport. The tired, weary men were kept there for two days in the blazing sun and cold nights. Gasoline tainted water and a bit of stale bread was our fare. On Christmas day we were taken to the barracks which by this time were encircled with barbed wire.

61 RICHARD S. CRENSHAW
    Chico, California
62 HUGH A. CURPHEY
    Grants Pass, Oregon
63 THOMAS J. BARBOUR
    Portland, Oregon
64 CARL H. CARLSEN
    Pocatello, Idaho
65 JOSEPH WARREN ADAMSON
    Twin Falls, Idaho
66 THOMAS W. BURKE
    Custer, South Dakota
67 THOMAS B. ARMITAGE
    Nampa, Idaho
68 EDWIN DEAN CHAMBERS
    Palacios, Texas
69 CHARLES R. DAVIS
    Boise, Idaho
70 NORMAN ALFRED ANDERSON
    Portland, Oregon
71 LOUIS A. ADAMSON (deceased)
    Twin Falls, Idaho
72 JOSEPH ASTARITA
    Brooklyn, New York
73 GERALD E. BOOTH
    Los Angeles, California
74 EDGAR-FRANKLIN BURNS
    Spokane, Washington
75 ARTHUR CHRISTY
    Boise, Idaho
76 MELVIN A. AUSTIN
    Portland, Oregon
77 JOHN CORAK
    Boise, Idaho
78 RAYFORD B. BLAKE
    Sheridan, Arkansas
79 DONLEY D. CHARD
    Midway, Utah
80 FRANK A. ARAMBARRI
    Gooding, Idaho
81 IVAN R. CARDEN
    La Junta, Colorado

Photographs of some of the interned civilians who had been employed by CPNAB at Wake, Guam and Cavite. These photos appeared in a 1945 publication, A Report to Returned CPNAB Prisoner of War Heroes and Their Dependents. Morrison-Knudsen Co.

Wake's captured American construction workers on their way to board the Nitta Maru. *Photo from a Japanese picture book.* USMC (#315174)

JAPANESE NAVAL REGULATIONS FOR PRISONERS OF WAR

Commander of the Prisoner Escort
Navy of the Great Japanese Empire

REGULATIONS FOR PRISONERS

1. The prisoners disobeying the following orders will be punished with immediate death:

    a. Those disobeying orders and instructions.
    b. Those showing a motion of antagonism and raising a sign of opposition.
    c. Those disordering the regulations by individualism, egoism, thinking only about yourself, rushing for your own goods.
    d. Those talking without permission and raising loud voices.
    e. Those walking and moving without order.
    f. Those carrying unnecessary baggage in embarking.
    g. those resisting mutually.
    h. Those touching the boat's materials, wires, electric lights, tools, switches, etc.
    i. Those climbing ladder without order.
    j. Those showing action of running away from the room or boat.
    k. Those trying to take more meal than given to them.
    l. Those using more than two blankets.

2. Since the boat is not well equipped and inside being narrow, food being scarce and poor you'll feel uncomfortable during the short time on the boat. Those losing patients and disobeying the regulation will be heavily punished for the reason of not being ....?

3. Be sure to finish your "Nature's Call", evacuate the bowels and urine before embarking.

4. Meals will be given twice a day. One plate only to one prisoner. The prisoners called by the guard will give out the meal quick as possible and honestly. The remaining prisoners will stay in their places quietly and wait for your plate. Those moving from their places reaching for your plate without order will be heavily punished. Same orders will be applied in handling plates after meal.

5. Toilet will be fixed at the four corners of the room. The buckets and cans will be placed. When filled up a guard will appoint a prisoner. The prisoner called will take the buckets to the center of the room. The buckets will be pulled up by the derrick and be thrown away. Toilet papers will be given. Everyone must cooperate to make the room sanitary. Those being careless will be punished.

6. Navy of the Great Japanese Empire will not try to punish you all with death. Those obeying all the rules and regulations, and believing the action and purpose of the Japanese Navy, cooperating with Japan in constructing the "New order of the Great Asia" which lead to the world's peace will be well treated.

The End

Japanese naval regulations given to each Wake captive as the prisoners boarded the Nitta Maru *on Jan. 12, 1942.*

Rogge Collection

In the hold of the Nita Maru sixteen days of hell were experienced. Beatings. Starvation. From sub-tropical weather to freezing January within forty-eight hours. The shock was terrific. After our debarkation at Woo Sung, China, we had to run all the way to the prison camp about four and a half miles away.

WHERE FREEDOM REIGNS

Maj. James P.S. Devereaux, Comm. U.S.M.C. Garrison at Wake Island: "After being south, it was cold spending the winter here. However, we were supplied with every convenience."

On the following three pages are photographs that appeared in the English-language propaganda magazine, Freedom, published by the Japanese in the spring of 1942. The bottom photo shows Cmdr. Cunningham (seated) in his Navy uniform, on board the Nitta Maru. Next to Cunningham is Dan Teters. Note the Japanese cameraman in the lower left corner. Devereux's name was misspelled in the article.   Jim Allen Collection

Radios were given to the prisoners in China, supposedly as a gesture of goodwill. The radios, however, could only be tuned to Japanese propaganda stations. Top photo, left to right: Col. W. Ashurst, commander of the North China Marines; Devereux and Raymond Rutledge, civilian captive from Wake. Bottom photo, top row, left to right: Dr. Kahn, Lt. Kessler, Lt. Lewis, Eng. Walsh, Lt. Barninger, Lt. Hanna and Lt. Kinney. Bottom row, left to right: unknown, Lt. Poindexter, Capt. Freuler, unknown, Col. Devereux.

Top photo: A picture supposedly showing good sanitary conditions at a POW camp in China. Of course, conditions were much worse than pictured. Middle photo: Cmdr. Cunningham making a recording at prison camp for broadcast to the United States. Bottom photo: Lt. Cmdr. Elmer B. Greey, the Navy civil engineer assigned to look after naval construction on Wake. The magazine quoted Greey as saying that conditions were good in camp, and that entertainment and recreation were provided.

Top: Photograph of Marines with two Japanese medical corpsmen, at the Kiangwan POW camp dispensary.
Stegmaier Collection

Bottom left: A Japanese medic at Kiangwan, China. He gave this photo to Carl Stegmaier, a Marine POW in the camp. Stegmaier Collection

Bottom right: Sgt. Maj. Tomekethi Takahashi, Imperial Japanese Army. Takahashi worked at a supply depot in Shanghai and treated with kindness the Wake POWs who worked for him. In early 1945 he was drafted into the kamikaze force but survived the war. Holmes Collection

On the next three pages is the art of Gurdon H. Wattles, a civilian captured on Wake. Wattles produced this work while in Woosung POW camp.

Dental Office
Woo Sung, China ©
Gurdon H. Wattles.

Galley
Woo Sung, China
Gurdon H. Wattles
November, 1942.

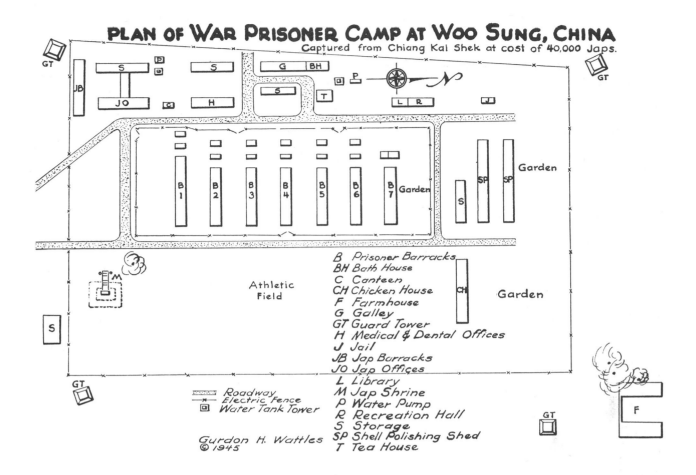

PLAN OF WAR PRISONER CAMP AT WOO SUNG, CHINA
Captured from Chiang Kai Shek at cost of 40,000 Japs.

Athletic Field

Garden

Garden

B   Prisoner Barracks
BH Bath House
C   Canteen
CH Chicken House
F   Farmhouse
G   Galley
GT Guard Tower
H   Medical & Dental Offices
J   Jail
JB Jap Barracks
JO Jap Offices
L   Library
M   Jap Shrine
P   Water Pump
R   Recreation Hall
S   Storage
SP Shell Polishing Shed
T   Tea House

Roadway
Electric Fence
Water Tank Tower

Gurdon H. Wattles
© 1945

Barber Shop
Woo Sung, China
Gurdon H. Wattles
1942 ©

Water Supply
Woo Sung, China

Gurdon H. Wattles
© 1942

Copy of a letter mailed by Maj. Devereux from the Shanghai POW camp in April 1943 and received by Devereux's son, Patrick, in December 1943. It was the first letter the boy received from his father in two years. The loss referred to in the letter was the death, in July 1942 in Washington, of Maj. Devereux's 27-year-old wife.

USMC

A Hero Writes to His Son

Dear Paddy:

Our loss must have indeed, been a shock to you; it was to me, We both loved her so much. I only wish that I could be with you but you are indeed fortunate to have your grand-parents to watch over you. I made a broadcast recording to you last fall. Do hope you received it in view of the fact that this is my first letter to you. Impossible to write more often.

In your mother's letter she said you were doing well in church and school. Keep up the good work. You will find both extremely necessary in later life. Since I can't do it, will you please ask your grandmother to have you given swimming and riding lessons. I do not care how well you are able to perform when I return but I do want you to like riding. You will have to help me school horses when we get our farm. Speaking of farming, I am learning quite a bit about it. We have text books and practical experience plus lots of advice.

Your mother wrote that you were "throwing your weight around" the post on account of the Wake Island Marines. They did quite well and I am proud of them but remember that it just so happened that we were there. Anyone else would have done the same. You must remember that the work done behind the lines is often more vital than that at the front.

You can see from the enclosed picture which was taken this winter that I am well as are most of us. Of course we would like to be going home and if an exchange is made, we should be among the first.

Please write as often as possible. My only letters were dated last June. I suppose you were able to be with your cousins for a while last summer and imagine that you will get to Chevy Chase this coming summer. As I have written before, I would like you to visit any of your cousins whenever it is possible.

Be sure and write everyone saying you have heard from me and give them my love.

Your affectionate father,

Paddy

Associated Press WIREPHOTO

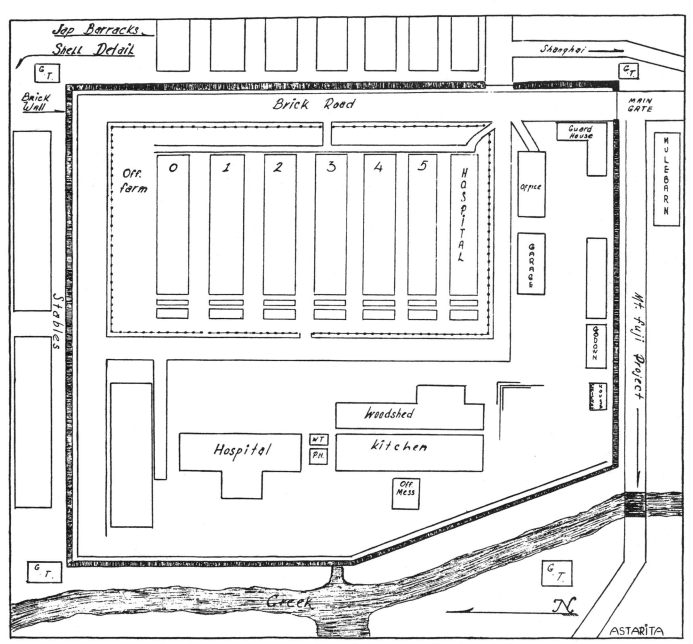

Exact plan of the Kiang Wan Prison Camp. Where men suffered, laughed, lived and died. This camp was just a short distance from Shanghai and the Chinese city sky-line could be seen as we marched out the gate to work.

A large project was the Woo Sung Canal which many men will remember. The hard work and freezing weather we had to contend with along with the skimpy amount of food was more than we could bear. Jap guards would stand at points of vantage such as Chinese graves (background) which were placed above the ground.

One of the largest details was the Mount Fuji project. The big stick was Ishihara (above) better known as the "Screaming Skull." A wild and vicious fanatic. He was head interpreter of the Shanghai camp. Hated by all, he would think nothing of smashing one in the adams apple with his riding crop or beating up our officers. In the background can be seen his pet project "Mt. Fuji."

The Marines called him "The Beast of the Far East." He died in 1956 while still in prison for war crimes against POWs.

When winter came we thought we would go mad with the cold. Marching up
and down the barracks trying to work up a bit of heat.

A large warehouse used as a POW camp in Fing Tai (Peking) China, June 1945.
Holmes Collection

Bottom right: This remarkable photo of T/Sgt. Charles Holmes was taken in the Shanghai War Prisoners Camp in November 1944 by a friendly Japanese guard while Holmes was on an out-of-camp work detail. In the photo he wears new coveralls and a cap, furnished by the International Red Cross, his first new clothes since December 1941. Holmes Collection

Looking across the harbor at Fusan (Pusan), Korea. In June 1945, POWs from Wake Island loaded salt aboard small steamers here which were bound for Japan. After a few days in Korea, the prisoners departed for Hokkaido, Japan, where they worked in coal mines until the end of the war.　　Holmes Collection

Living conditions were horrible and it rained almost every day in the POW camp in Fusan, Korea, June 1945.　　Holmes Collection

Marines worked in this Japanese coal mine on Hokkaido Island until their rescue on Sept. 16, 1945 from Hokodate POW camp #3.
　　Holmes Collection

Hokodate #3 POW camp on Hokkaido Island at the end of the war. On the left is a pole erected by the prisoners to fly an American flag made from red, white and blue air-drop parachutes.
Holmes Collection

Wake Island POWs on their freedom flight on Sept. 16, 1945, from Sapporo, Hokkaido, to Atsugi NAS, Japan. Holmes Collection

The Yamata steel mill, Japan, where many Wake Islanders worked in 1945.
Bud Sager, Lewiston, Idaho

FROM MAIN GATE LOOKING AT W.P. BARRACKS

The following photographs show the Shanghai War Prisoners Camp immediately after the camp was abandoned at the end of the war. The pictures were taken by soldiers who went back to the camp to exhume bodies of the dead captives. Holmes Collection

TOILETS

SGT GUTHIRES GRAVE
Ph. SGt BECK.

ENTERANG TO CEMETARY

CEMETARY

X-HOME

Devereux inspects a picture of his young son, Paddy, whom he had not seen in almost four years. Devereux was on Guam, heading back to the United States after he had been liberated from prison camp where he had spent 44 months.
USN (Navy News)

Devereux arrives at the Naval Air Station, Pearl Harbor, on Sept. 20, 1945, on his way back to the United States.
NA (#80-G-383293)

Cunningham holds a press conference upon his return from prison camps. His wife was also present.
NA (#80-G-70886)

The Japanese Occupation of Wake
Dec. 23, 1941 - Sept. 7, 1945

The Japanese occupied Wake Island for 44 months —from the American surrender of the island in late 1941 until two days after Japan formally surrendered the war in September 1945.* During those 44 months the island withstood heavy American bombardment, but at a cost of over 2,000 Japanese.

After taking Wake, the Japanese wanted to make the island a defensive stronghold. To this end, they utilized what was left of the American defense installations and they retained on the island 98 American civilians who could run heavy equipment to reconstruct defenses, taking the rest of the Americans off the island in early 1942.

Japan's first priority for Wake Island was to develop air strength and airfield facilities. Just after the takeover, Japan based her first air unit on Wake—a Navy bombing unit of 10 "Betty" bombers. Japanese fighter planes were stationed on the island in early 1943, with Japanese air strength on Wake reaching a peak of about 55 to 60 aircraft. By the end of 1943, however, all Japanese aircraft on the island had been destroyed.

Before the first American attacks on the island, Japan's defenses there consisted of 68 guns—eight coastal defense guns, seven dual-purpose guns and 53 anti-aircraft guns. About one-third of these eventually were destroyed by American bombers.

The Japanese garrison on Wake was commanded by Rear Adm. Shigimatsu Sakaibara, I.J.N., who took over the command in December 1942 and who would surrender the island 33 months later. The original garrison under Sakaibara's command was augmented in early 1943 with 600 additional army troops, and another 1,000 men were transported to the island in January 1944. In all, about 4,400 Japanese troops were stationed on Wake, but by the

time of the island's surrender, deaths from air raids and malnutrition had reduced the number to 1,242.

The rapid military buildup on Wake turned out to be something of a wasted effort on the part of the Japanese. For the most part, the war passed by the island, especially after the Battle of Midway in June 1942. By 1943-44, the rebuilt American fleet had turned most of the Pacific into an "American lake," but Wake remained in enemy hands. With its relentless island-hopping drive towards the Japanese mainland, America saw no reason to expend the time and troops to retake the isolated island that was now in the backwater of the American fleet.

The Americans, however, did not altogether ignore Wake Island. On Feb. 24, 1942, just two months after the island's fall, American forces executed their first carrier strike against Wake, using planes flown from the *Enterprise*, and on July 8, 1943, eight B-24s from Midway made the first land-based strike against the island.

Another major carrier raid occurred on Oct. 5-6, 1943, and in the first five months of 1944, 966 sorties were flown against Wake, dropping 1,079 tons of bombs. September and October of 1944 brought repeated strikes against Wake, continuing through the first part of 1945. The last air raid against Wake took place on Aug. 13, 1945, and was made by Marine Corps aircraft.

Japanese sources estimated that about 47 American planes were shot down during these air raids. Most of the downed planes were carrier-borne, with the exception of one B-24 and one PB4Y.

Besides the air attacks, the island faced continual bombardment by American ships that were steaming past. In fact, the island served as a target for gunnery training by American vessels.

By late 1943 or early 1944, the Japanese probably had written off the island, but they still had to supply Wake whenever the American blockade could be breached. The last Japanese supply ship to Wake arrived from Kwajalein on Jan. 1, 1944; after that, only a few submarines managed to run the blockade and bring supplies. Even that scant support ended on June 28, 1945.

Without regular supplies, the Japanese battled malnutrition. Furthermore, constant bombardment from air and sea reduced the garrison to relative impotence and had driven the Japanese underground. In July 1945, the Japanese hospital ship *Taramago Maru*, after being intercepted and released by the Americans, carried 970 sick and wounded from Wake, an indication of the deteriorating condition of the island's garrison. In all, approximately 725 Japanese on Wake died from air and naval bombardment and 1,300 died from sickness and malnutrition during the 44-month occupation.

The nature of the Japanese occupation of the island and the American missions against Wake is best summed up in the conclusion of the Strategic Bombing Report on the Reduction of Wake Island.**

At the time of its surrender to American forces in September 1945, Wake Island, originally conceived of by the Japanese as a key base in their program of expansion toward the east, had become a lonely outpost, severed of all communication with the homeland, with negligible defenses and a dying garrison. Of the air base, few facilities and no planes remained. The defensive position had been deprived of 20 percent of its fire power and, in any event, was impotent when manned by a garrison which was capable of working only a few hours a day and had long given up normal operations.

The offensive and defensive capabilities of Wake could not have been more effectively reduced had it been the object of sustained American campaign or invasion. Yet, in effect, operations against the island were desultory in character. The first fierce attacks during the period of the Gilberts and Marshall campaigns had completely nullified the offensive value of the base. The period that followed was mainly one of attrition and blockade which reduced both the defensive ability and the defensive will of the island.

The Japanese garrison on Wake Island was not forced to surrender. However, American airpower, by assisting in blockade and by bombing and machine gunning, was largely responsible for reducing the island's defenses to such as state of ineffectiveness that a successful landing could have been made with a minimum effort—a fact attested to by the Island Commander, who stated that by June 1945 his forces could no longer have repelled an invasion.

USS Northampton *under attack by a Japanese seaplane during the Feb. 24, 1942, raid on Wake.* USN (#NH50947)

*The Japanese changed the names of the islands to Ottori (Wake), Habe (Peale) and Ashi (Wilkes).

**See Bibliography.

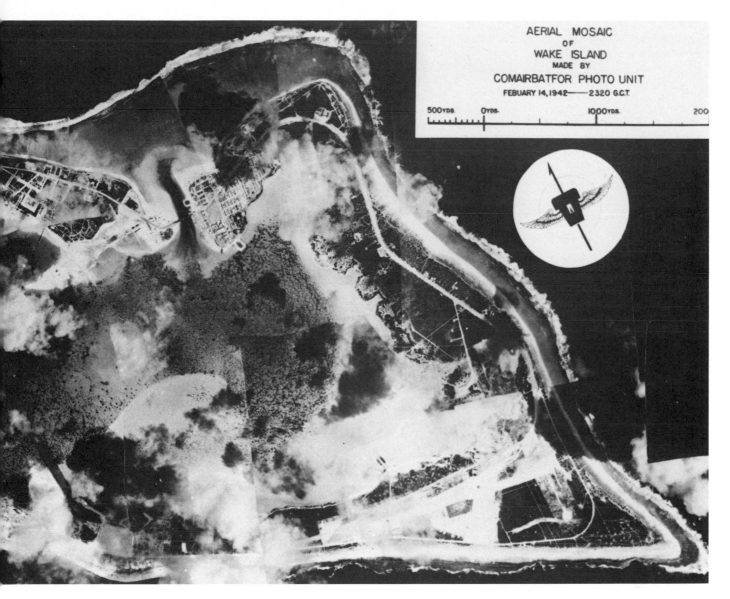

AERIAL MOSAIC
OF
WAKE ISLAND
MADE BY
COMAIRBATFOR PHOTO UNIT
FEBUARY 14,1942———2320 G.C.T.

500YDS.   0YDS.   1000YDS.   200

View of a Japanese patrol boat under attack by gunfire from the USS Balch *and* USS Maury *and aircraft from the* USS Enterprise *during the Feb. 24, 1942 raid.*

Top: A Japanese school paper, apparently published for the study of the English language, had as its lead article a story on the defense of Wake Island.

David Aiken, Dallas, Texas

Bottom left and right: Japanese prisoners taken by Task Force 16 after its attack on Wake Island. The prisoners were rescued after their patrol boat was sunk by 5'' shell fire. NA (#80-G-2001 and #80-G-2003)

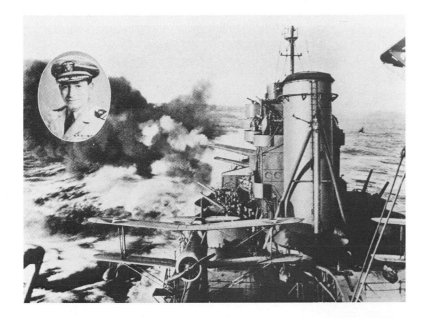

Main batteries of the USS Salt Lake City *open up on Wake on Feb. 24, 1942. Also pictured is the cruiser's captain, Ellis Zacharias.*
Author's Collection

USS San Francisco *bombarding Wake on Oct. 5, 1943. The* USS New Orleans *is next astern. The photo was taken from the* USS Minneapolis. NA (#80-G-55238)

A Japanese vessel burns in the Wake Island channel after the Oct. 5 raid. USN (#NH4779)

This much publicized photo shows a Douglas TBD torpedo bomber flying over Wake in 1943.
Author's Collection

Cruisers protecting a carrier during the Feb. 24, 1942 attack on Wake.   NA (#80-G-17021)

Six Navy airmen who were shot down in the raid on Wake on Oct. 5-6, 1943. Left to right: Aviation Ordnance Mate 2nd Class Paul T. Ronilla; Lt. j.g. William B. McCarthy; Lt. Harold J. Kicker; Lt. Cmdr. Mark A. Grant, USN; Lt. j.g. Richard C. Johnson; and Ensign Murray H. Tyler. The six men were adrift in life rafts in the vicinity of Wake for intervals ranging from 35 minutes to four days and three nights. They were rescued by a U.S. submarine which had lurked near the Japanese base after the raid in the hope of picking up survivors of plane crashes.   NA (#80-G-44073)

Fuel storage tanks set afire by American planes and warships on Oct. 5-6, 1943. Thirty-one planes on the ground were destroyed in this raid.   NA (#208-16790)

The March 28, 1944, raid on Wake. Between January and May 1944, Americans flew 966 sorties over the island, dropping 1,079 tons of bombs.   NA (#208-N-23911)

Japanese installations being attacked on June 20, 1945, in one of the last raids of the war on Wake.   NA (#80-G-490022)

The Japanese Surrender

On Sept. 4, 1945, two days after Japan formally surrendered in Tokyo Bay, Rear Adm. Shigematsu Sakaibara, I.J.N., surrendered Wake Island to Brig. Gen. L.H.M. Sanderson, USMC. Sanderson represented Rear Adm. W.K. Harrill, the commander of the Marshalls-Gilberts Surrender and Occupation Command.

The American occupation party had arrived off Wake earlier that same day. The party consisted of three destroyer escorts of Com Cont Div 11—the *USS Lehardy* (DE 20), the *USS Charles R. Greer* (DE 23), and the *USS Levy* (DE 162), the ship aboard which the surrender was signed.

Three days after the signing, Americans landed on Wake. Col. Walter Bayler, the last man off Wake on Dec. 20, 1941, was the first American to set foot on the island in 44 months. A flag ceremony was held with both Japanese and Americans in attendance; the island was officially in American hands again.

The occupying forces found the Japanese enlisted men in advanced stages of malnutrition, and men were dying daily. By comparison, the officers were in good condition.

The island had been completely devastated by the constant air and naval raids, and the surrendered Japanese were put to work repairing some of the damage of the past four years. In November 1945 the 1,200 Japanese were taken off the island, thus ending the saga of Wake.

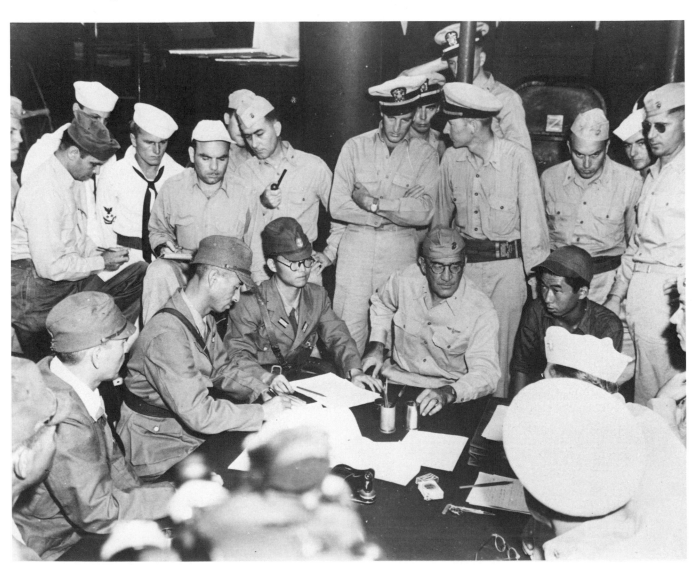

Signing the formal surrender of Wake Island on Sept. 4, 1945, on board the USS Levy. Rear Adm. Shigematsu Sakaibara, commander of the garrison, signs the surrender document. Japanese left to right: Maj. Masao Yoshimiza, Col. Shigehara Chikamori, Sakaibara, Paymaster Lt. P. Hisao Napasato, and Sgt. Iarry Watanabe of Honolulu, official interpreter at the surrender. Seated, accepting the surrender, is Brig. Gen. Lawson H.M. Sanderson, commander of the 4th Marine Air Wing. Col. Walter Bayler (center with pipe) was the last American off Wake in December 1941.

USMC (#336687)

Rear Adm. Sakaibara.
NA (#80-G-346822)

As a Marine bugler plays "Colors," the Stars and Stripes are hoisted over Wake Island in September 1945. The Japanese official at the extreme right is Rear Adm. Shigematsu Sakaibara.   USMC (#133686)

Col. Walter Bayler, the last man off Wake Island in 1941, is the first American to set foot on the island after its surrender in 1945.
USMC (#133688)

USS Levy *(DE 162)* NA (#80-G-66991)

The first plane to land on Wake Island since its capture, a Marine transport of Squadron 352 takes off from the airstrip that the Japanese had repaired.
USMC (#133851)

Japanese sailors line up before leaving Wake aboard the hospital ship MS Hikawa Maru *on Nov. 1, 1945.*

NA (#208AA-286P-3)

On their way home, Japanese personnel board the MS Hikawa Maru lying off Wake, Nov. 1, 1945. Ten of these men had come to Wake during the initial Japanese landing on Dec. 23, 1941.   NA (#208-PU-286P-6)

A Japanese bows as he passes the grave of American contractor Will Miles, who died on July 15, 1942. This photograph was taken after the Japanese surrender.

NA (#208-N4-3923PPA)

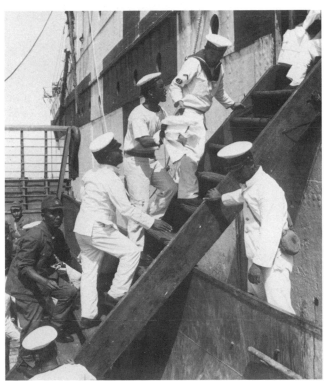

The photographs on the following four pages were taken after the Japanese surrender of the island on Sept. 4, 1945.

Small Japanese artillery, captured on Wake, en route to the United States.   NA (#80-G-346844)

Japanese hospital operating room and some items captured in 1941 from Americans.
NA (#80-G-346819)

Japanese senior medical officer examining malnutrition cases.   NA (#80-G-346811)

Japanese 8'' coastal gun on Pigeon Point.
NA (#80-G-346846)

Remains of barracks building. NA (#80-G-346845)

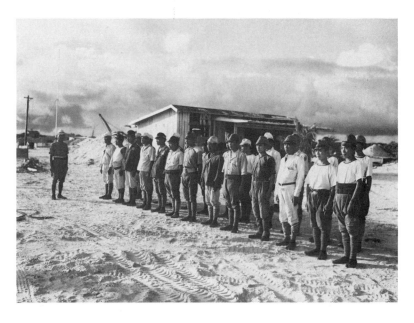

A Japanese work party musters before beginning the morning's tasks. NA (#80-G-346806)

Japanese living quarters had been dug into the sand. NA (#80-G-346841)

Members of a working party at their noon rice meal. NA (#80-G-346803)

Wrecked Zero aircraft. NA (#80-G-346823)

Takeo Endo (center), one of the original invaders of Wake in 1941, was still on the island at its surrender in 1945.   NA (#80-G-338695)

Small Japanese tanks brought to the island from Manchuria.   NA (#80-G-346843)

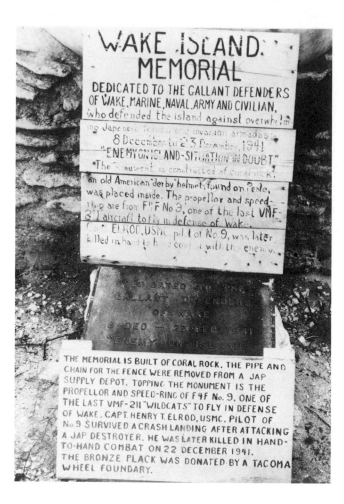

This monument to the defenders of Wake Island was built by Lt. Marshall K. Phillips, USCG officer in charge of the island's LORAN station in 1955. The engine cowling has since been removed and placed in a Wildcat display at the National Air and Space Museum in Washington, D.C. A new memorial has since been built.

USMC (#A420788 and #A410507)

Legacy of Wake Island

Wake Island took on an important role in post-war American defense plans. It became a refueling stop for trans-Pacific military flights, as well as a navigational and weather station.

In 1947, the Navy turned over the island to the Federal Aviation Administration. A modern, 9,800-foot runway capable of handling the largest aircraft was built on Wake, and this facility was used to service military and civilian aircraft until the early 1970s.

After 1962, the FAA assumed civil administration of the island. For the next ten years, the Air Force operated its refueling station while the FAA managed the island's airport, air navigation aids, utilities, roads, living quarters, mess facilities, maintenance and repair shops, public health services, schools, and police and fire services.

Also in 1962, Pan Am, which had returned to the island after the war, started using a new passenger terminal at Wake. The airline made regular stops at the island until 1971.

In the 1960s, the U.S. Coast Guard operated a long-range navigational aid station (LORAN) on Peale Island, and the U.S. Weather Bureau maintained a weather station on the atoll to monitor the Central Pacific area.

In 1972, the FAA turned over civil administration of the atoll to the U.S. Air Force, but the FAA continued to operate the air facilities for another year, when the administration left the island. After 1973, there was no need for the air facilities on Wake because modern jets could cross the Pacific without refueling.

Today (1983) Wake has a population of about 80. The Air Force still maintains a small station on the atoll, but uses the airfield only for emergencies.

The Wake Island battle is not the only significant event to occur on the atoll in recent history. On Oct. 15, 1950, Wake was the scene of an important meeting between President Harry S. Truman and Gen. Douglas MacArthur. Other recent events include the devastating typhoons that hit Wake in 1952 and again in 1967.

The battle's legacy, of course, includes the memorials built both on the atoll and elsewhere. A 200-seat chapel was constructed in 1966 near the passenger terminal building on Wake. The chapel honors the dead of all wars, but particularly the men who defended Wake during World War II.

Earlier, another memorial had been constructed on the island. In 1955, Lt. Marshall K. Phillips, in charge of Wake's LORAN station, built a monument dedicated to Capt. Henry Elrod and the defenders of Wake. The monument included the propeller and speed ring from Elrod's plane #9. These pieces were removed in 1964 and incorporated in an F4F display at the National Air and Space Museum in Washington D.C. A more permanent monument was later constructed on the atoll.

The Japanese also have honored the battle of Wake. In 1957, Japan Air Lines built a memorial on the island that is inscribed with a simple message—"May Peace Prevail on the Waters of the Pacific Forever."

Wake Island memorials are found elsewhere, too. A Wake Island display can be seen at the Marine Corps Aviation Museum in Quantico, Va. This display consists of an F4F-4, a model of the Wake Island Memorial, Elrod's Medal of Honor and other medals, and a diorama of the Dec. 23 invasion built by students of the class of 1985, Gilbert Junior High School, Gilbert, Ariz., under the guidance of Glen Frakes.

In 1980, a memorial to the Wake defenders was placed in VFW Park in Briston, Okla., and in 1983, one was placed at the Marine Corps Recruit Depot, San Diego, Calif. A memorial to the men killed on Wake is at the Punchbowl Cemetery in Honolulu and the battle of Wake also will be honored in the form of a guided missile frigate. The ship will be commissioned in 1985 and named for Capt. Henry Elrod.

Nor have the survivors of Wake forgotten their place in history. Shortly after regaining their freedom, the civilians captured on Wake held their first reunion, in Boise, Idaho, on Dec. 7, 1945. Originally named the Workers of Wake Island, the group was reorganized in the mid-1950s and the name changed to the Survivors of Wake, Guam and Cavite Inc. The group has a membership of about 350 and it publishes a newsletter, the Little Wig Wag.

The Marines also have a Wake survivors organization that holds reunions annually. For many years the Wake Island Defenders reunions took place in Oklahoma, but recently they have been moved to other locations. The Marines' group also publishes a newsletter, the Wig Wag.

Gen. A.A. Vandegrift, commandant of the Marine Corps, presents the Medal of Honor on Nov. 8, 1946, to Capt. Elizabeth J. Elrod, also of the Marine Corps, the widow of the man who won the medal. USMC

Beached Suwa Maru *on Wake in 1951. The 10,000-ton merchant ship was hit by two torpedoes in the summer of 1943.* Pan Am Collection

Japanese 8'' gun, brought from Hong Kong, on Peacock Point, 1951.
Pan Am Collection

Japanese dugout on Wake, 1951.
Pan Am Collection

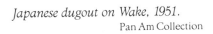

This Japanese blockhouse was still standing in 1953. Pan Am Collection

The Movie "Wake Island"

Just four months after the island's fall, filming began on the movie "Wake Island." Although its production was delayed a few weeks on the slim hope that the island would be recaptured, the movie was the first Hollywood film after the Pearl Harbor attack that attempted to portray accurately American fighting men.

The Paramount Pictures film was directed by ex-Marine John Farrow with a screenplay by W.R. Burnett and Frank Butler. It featured some notable film actors of the day: McDonald Carey, Robert Preston, William Bendix, Walter Abel, Rod Cameron and Barbara Britton.

For 30 days, crews filmed at a mock-up of the island at California's Salton Sea. Morrison-Knudsen Co., the company that had worked on Wake, was hired to reproduce the island's facilities. Because Japanese-Americans were interned, Filipinos and Chinese were trained to portray the Japanese soldiers. About 2,000 extras participated in the film.

The Marine Corps loaned six F4F-3s for the filming, while five Ryan SCWs were used to simulate Japanese ASM "Claude" fighters. Because of wartime restrictions, only 30 tons of explosives were available for bomb explosions.

When the make-believe Japanese planes flew over for their simulated bomb runs, local residents and the area's anti-aircraft batteries had to be warned in order to avoid alarm and the possibility that the planes would be fired upon.

The film, which was first shown before 2,000 Marines at Quantico in August 1942, was very popular and had a great impact on the promotion of the war effort. It also received three Oscar nominations.

Paramount gave bronze plaques to high-ranking Marine officers around the country in honor of the film. The only civilian to receive one of these plaques was Col. Devereux's 9-year-old son, James P.S. Devereux II, who received the award in the office of his grandfather, Col. John P. Welch, commanding officer of the Richmond Quartermaster Depot.

Scenes of the 1942 filming of the movie "Wake Island" at the Salton Sea. Academy of Motion Pictures Arts and Sciences

Wake's 9,800-foot runway is now used only occasionally. FAA

In the 1960s and early 1970s Wake was a major refueling stop for military planes flying to and from the Far East. FAA

View of the Wake Island display and the F4F-4 Wildcat at the Marine Corps Aviation Museum in Quantico, Va. The plane is one of two Grumman-built Wildcats known to exist and is the only one remaining in this country. It was acquired in September 1968 from Seattle Community College, and it bears bureau number 12114 (830 323-0R). The photo shows the diorama of Wake that was constructed under the direction of Glen Frakes by students of the class of 1985, Gilbert Junior High School, Gilbert, Ariz. A propeller from one of the original Wake Island Wildcats is also on display. Until 1964 the propeller was part of the memorial on Wake Island.

Marine Corps Aviation Museum

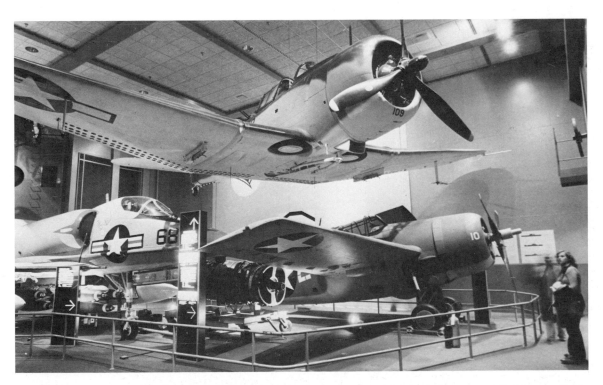

An F4F-4 on display in the Sea-Air Operations Gallery of the National Air and Space Museum, Washington, D.C.

National Air and Space Museum

Present-day memorial to Americans who fought on Wake in 1941.
U.S. Air Force

Japanese war memorial, built in 1957, honoring those who died on Wake. Holmes Collection

The 1978 reunion of the Marine Corps Defenders of Wake Island, in Oklahoma City, Okla. Holmes Collection

Civilian survivors of Wake at the 1980 reunion picnicked at the historic mining town of Idaho City, Idaho. The reunion was held in Boise, Idaho.
L.S. McCurry, Boise, Idaho

Lt. Col. Charles Harrison, captured on Wake Island, had the misfortune of being captured by the Chinese in 1950 near Changjin Reservoir during the Korean War.   Holmes Collection

Initials of an American civilian POW who was left on Wake after most prisoners had been removed on Jan. 12, 1942. The prisoner was executed on Oct. 7, 1943.
Holmes Collection

Wake Island memorial at the Punch-bowl Cemetery, Honolulu, Hawaii.
Bud Sager, Lewiston, Idaho

Front and back of a memorial erected in 1980 at VFW Park in Bristow, Okla.   Holmes Collection

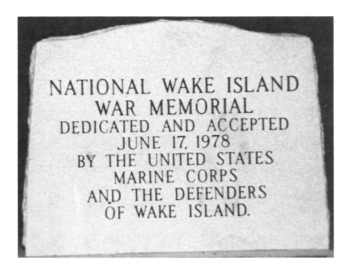

NATIONAL WAKE ISLAND
WAR MEMORIAL
DEDICATED AND ACCEPTED
JUNE 17, 1978
BY THE UNITED STATES
MARINE CORPS
AND THE DEFENDERS
OF WAKE ISLAND.

WAKE ISLAND POW'S
12-23-41 TO 9-10-45

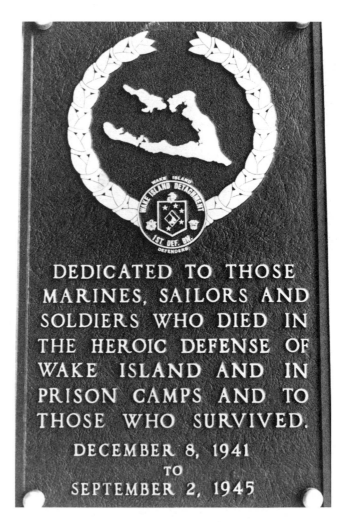

DEDICATED TO THOSE
MARINES, SAILORS AND
SOLDIERS WHO DIED IN
THE HEROIC DEFENSE OF
WAKE ISLAND AND IN
PRISON CAMPS AND TO
THOSE WHO SURVIVED.
DECEMBER 8, 1941
TO
SEPTEMBER 2, 1945

Plaque dedicated on Aug. 10, 1983, to the Wake Island Defenders by Maj. Gen. W.H. Rice, USMC, the commanding general of the Marine Corps Recruit Depot, San Diego, Calif. The plaque is placed in Building 31 at the depot.   Robert Curry, Hemet, Calif.

Seven-inch gun moved from Singapore to Wake in 1942.

Adm. Shigematsu Sakaibara's headquarters on Wake Island.

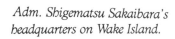

Japanese bunker, west shore of Wilkes. Holmes Collection

Appendix

TASK ORGANIZATION OF JAPANESE FORCES ATTACKING WAKE, 8-13 DECEMBER, 1941

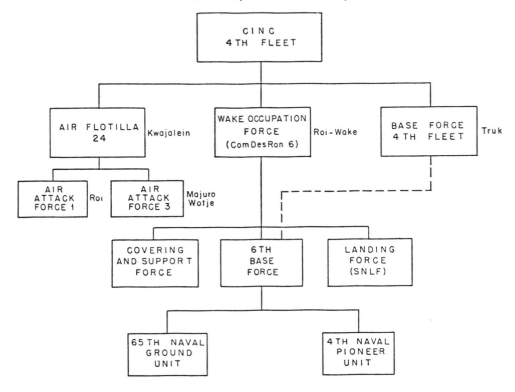

TASK ORGANIZATION OF JAPANESE FORCES SEIZURE OF WAKE, 23 DECEMBER, 1941

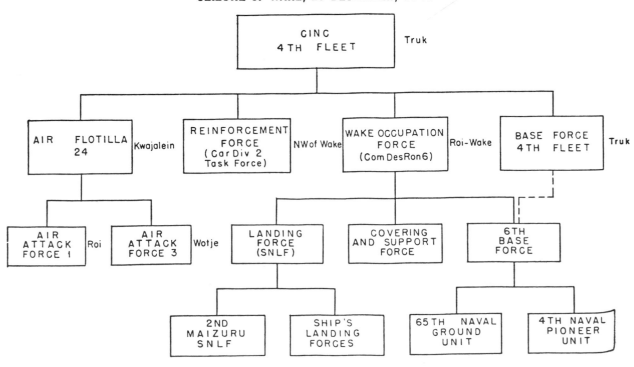

COMMAND STRUCTURE OF U. S. FORCES INVOLVED IN THE DEFENSE OF WAKE

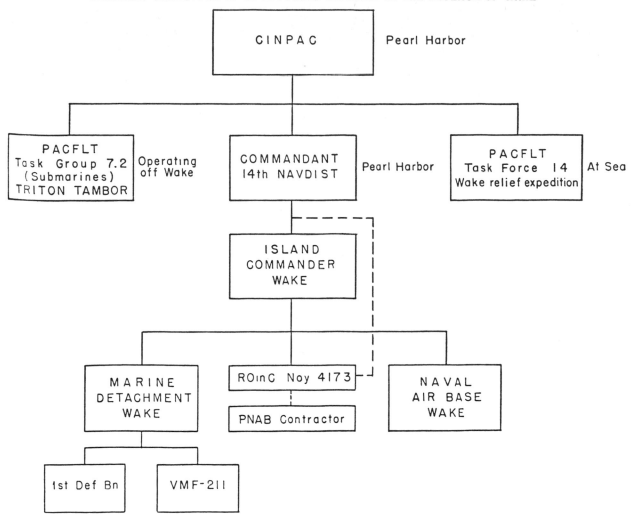

The White House
Washington
5 January 1942

Citation by
THE PRESIDENT OF THE UNITED STATES
of

The Wake detachment of the 1st Defense Battalion, U.S. Marine Corps, under command of Major James P.S. Devereux, U.S. Marines

and

Marine Fighting Squadron 211 of Marine Aircraft Group 21, under command of Major Paul A. Putnam, U.S. Marines

The courageous conduct of the officers and men of these units, who defended Wake Island against an overwhelming superiority of enemy air, sea, and land attacks from December 8 to 22, 1941, has been noted with admiration by their fellow countrymen and the civilized world, and will not be forgotten so long as gallantry and heroism are respected and honored. These units are commended for their devotion to duty and splendid conduct at their battle stations under most adverse conditions. With limited defensive means against attacks in great force, they manned their shore installations and flew their aircraft so well that five enemy warships were either sunk or severely damaged, many hostile planes shot down, and an unknown number of land troops destroyed.

DECORATIONS and COMMENDATIONS

NAVY CROSS: HILL, CHARLES C., PFC., USMC,
(PLANT CITY, FLORIDA)

"For extraordinary heroism while serving as Acting Leader of a .30 Caliber Machine Gun Section of Battery I, First Defense Battalion, during the defense of Wake Island against enemy Japanese forces, from 8 to 23 December 1941. Instantly taking over when his section leader was unable to continue, Private First Class Hill skillfully reorganized his seven-man section, which included four civilians unfamiliar with the weapons, and directed the barrage of his batteries. Blazing away with his two guns, he raked the enemy with blistering fire, repeatedly drove back fiendish attacks, and cleared the Japanese from his section of the beach. Faced with tremendous odds when two destroyers beached about one hundred and fifty yards from him and began to disgorge armed troops, he unhesitatingly moved forward to take up a dangerously exposed position and enfilade the enemy lines. Oblivious of the danger from the opposing superior firepower, he fought his guns coolly and accurately, shattering the oncoming lines with his withering fire, killing approximately one hundred and fifty Japanese, and forcing countless others to withdraw. His inspiring leadership, courage under fire, and unfaltering devotion to duty reflect the highest credit upon Private First Class Hill and the United States Naval Services."

Bibliography

Bayler, Walter L.J., *Last Man Off Wake Island*, Bobbs-Merrill, Indianapolis, 1943.

Cunningham, Winfield Scott, *Wake Island Command*, Little, Brown & Co., Boston, 1961.

Devereux, Col. James P.S., *The Story of Wake Island*, J.B. Lippincott, Philadelphia, 1947.

Heinl, Lt. Col. R.D. Jr., *The Defense of Wake*, Historical Section, Division of Public Information, Headquarters U.S. Marine Corps, 1947.

Hough, Frank O.; Ludwig, Verle E.; and Shaw, Henry I., Jr., USMC Historical Section. *Pearl Harbor to Guadalcanal*. History of U.S. Marine Corps Operations in World War II, vol. 1. Washington D.C.: Government Printing Office, 1958.

Morison, Samuel Eliot, *The Rising Sun in the Pacific, 1931-April 1942*, History of the United States Naval Operations in World War II, Vol. 3, Little, Brown & Co., Boston, 1963.

Schultz, Duane, *Wake Island, The Heroic Gallant Fight*, St. Martin's Press, New York, 1978.

Plus numerous magazine articles, official reports, personal interviews.

About the Author

Stan Cohen, the author of *Enemy on Island. Issue in Doubt.*, has been interested in military history, especially World War II, since his grade school days in Charleston, W.Va. Though he was trained as a geologist at West Virginia University, he now conducts a full-time publishing business. He has published 34 books since 1976, including 21 he has authored or co-authored. His military research has produced: *The Forgotten War*, a pictorial history of World War II in Alaska and northwestern Canada; *East Wind Rain*, a pictorial history of the Pearl Harbor attack; *The Civil War in West Virginia*, a pictorial history; *Military and Trading Posts of Montana*, and *Destination: Tokyo*, a pictorial history of Doolittle's raid. He has also published books on the American warships *Enterprise, West Virginia, Pennsylvania, California* and *Lexington*, and on the British liner *Queen Mary*. He resides with his wife, Anne, and sons, John and Andy, in Missoula, Mont., his home for the past 22 years.